Philosophy of Qohelet

Philosophy of Qohelet

A Critical Analysis of Existentialism

JOEL STEELE

RESOURCE *Publications* • Eugene, Oregon

PHILOSOPHY OF QOHELET
A Critical Analysis of Existentialism

Copyright © 2021 Joel Steele. All rights reserved. Except for brief quotations in critical publications or reviews, no part of this book may be reproduced in any manner without prior written permission from the publisher. Write: Permissions, Wipf and Stock Publishers, 199 W. 8th Ave., Suite 3, Eugene, OR 97401.

Resource Publications
An Imprint of Wipf and Stock Publishers
199 W. 8th Ave., Suite 3
Eugene, OR 97401

www.wipfandstock.com

PAPERBACK ISBN: 978-1-6667-0204-0
HARDCOVER ISBN: 978-1-6667-0205-7
EBOOK ISBN: 978-1-6667-0206-4

04/07/21

TO MY FAMILY
Jami, Braiden, Kayce, and Grant

The Western world has lost its civil courage, both as a whole and separately, in each country, each government, each political party, and, of course, in the United Nations. Such a decline in courage is particularly noticeable among the ruling groups and the intellectual elite, causing an impression of loss of courage by the entire society.

—Aleksandr Solzhenitsyn

Contents

Preface — ix

Introduction — xi

Chapter 1 | Existentialism — 1

Chapter 2 | Distorted Courage, the Great Regression, and Morality — 11

Chapter 3 | Historical Context and Background — 20

Chapter 4 | Textual Analysis — 30

Chapter 5 | Applications, Imposters, and Fearing God — 36

Bibliography — 45

Index — 49

Preface

THIS RESEARCH COMPARES AND contrasts various existential philosophies pertaining to the human condition and its purpose. It specifically focuses on the Old Testament book of Ecclesiastes. It exposes the source and essence of the philosophy. A linguistic approach combined with known historical conquests were used to argue against Greek influences on the Hebrew text of Ecclesiastes. Original sources were extracted from ancient writings to disclose existential arguments. Key word studies demonstrate the origination of translated words and their meanings within the context of passages. *Nicomachean Ethics* and *The Nature of the Gods* regarding virtue, courage, and the necessity of an eternal source were examined as they relate to the subject from a Western worldview. For secondary sources, the utilization of scholarly commentaries assisted in constructing a historiography of literature disclosing contributions made by a diversified range of scholars. Digital archives were helpful in substantiating the validity of original sources. The intended contributions of this research are to disclose that without objectifiable references society becomes a cluster of subjective abominations susceptible to a miserable existence, a slow descent into madness, "a chasing after the wind." To escape this vanity something eternal must exist. Nevertheless, humanity must confront the abyss that Nietzsche struggled with in his version of existential philosophy to find meaning in this life. Indeed, when gazing into an abyss the abyss gazes back into humanity, but rather than surrendering one's autonomy to the meaningless void, individuals

Preface

should determine the inherent value of their life. Otherwise, death, as Qohelet recognized, has a grip on the individual long before they actually die. Secular philosophical existentialism appears to be deficient in this area. The secondary contribution will be to demonstrate that the author of the text was not influenced by Hellenistic thought. It was the development of Western philosophy pertaining to ethics, integrated with Christian theology, which originated and transcended from the Old Testament disclosing the source for humanity's morality. It is these writings, from Qohelet and other Old Testament passages, that are foundational for producing significant contributions to objective moral philosophy.

Introduction

THE BOOK OF ECCLESIASTES is attributed to a descendant of David—Solomon. The word in the opening verse "vanity" is perhaps the most important word for the entire book. The term occurs four times in the verse (once in plural form) and thirty-seven times in the book. The term "vanity of vanities" is a superlative construction, like "holy of holies."[1] The reality of the human condition and the ability to enjoy life is brought into focus by the author through analyzing various engagements on earth that all seem to have little significance, vanity. The Hebrew word הֶבֶל (*hevel*), is defined by Strong as: "emptiness or vanity; figuratively, something transitory and unsatisfactory; often used as an adverb: —x altogether, vain, vanity."[2] The Hebrew word has been further explored by scholars and determined to essentially mean "mere breath."[3] Moreover, many readers assume Solomon is the author of the book. However, the opening verse only referred to him as "son of David." This opens the possibility that the author is merely from the Davidic line. Still, there are passages that indicate he is indeed Solomon, or, at least, this is what the author wants the reader to believe. There is much uncertainty regarding the title of the book as well. The Septuagint translators decided on "Ecclesiastes" as the title because it means "the one who assembles."[4] Nevertheless, because of the discrepan-

---

1. *New Oxford Annotated Bible*, 947.
2. Strong, "Hebrew Strong's Dictionary."
3. Alter, *Hebrew Bible*, 3:675.
4. Alter, *Hebrew Bible*, 3:673.

INTRODUCTION

cies in the Hebrew translation, many scholars use the untranslated Hebrew word "Qohelet."[5] The author recognized that everything accomplished by humans "under the sun" lacks meaning at the end of one's life. To escape vanity, humans must remember their creator, embrace those close to them, find enjoyment in their toil (work,) and live a virtuous life by fearing or acknowledging God. The word is used a final time (perhaps a final warning) at the end of the book. Interestingly, the phrase is repeated nearly verbatim to the opening: "Vanity of vanities, says the Teacher; all is vanity" (Eccl 12:8). It is this quasi-narrative on the human condition, which the author vexingly contemplated, that motivates this research. It utilizes comparative literature on secular philosophic ideology to demonstrate humanity's inherent meaning is inefficient without an eternal guide. Jean-Paul Sartre once quipped, "Man is a useless passion." This statement is true if humanity has no objectifiable reference by which to be guided.

ANCIENT PHILOSOPHY

Certain philosophers from antiquity—Greek and Roman—have attempted to provide their constituents with a moral code, an objectifiable reference to live by that would enable them to make ethical decisions. Thus, a moral philosophy was developed. These philosophical concepts were so influential that they would prevail far beyond antiquity and extend into the modern era. They are the center of philosophical issues pertaining to ethics and morality. By 77 BC, Cicero, the Roman statesmen turned philosopher, had acquired a firm grasp of Hellenistic philosophy through discussions with their leading scholars.[6] Cicero's philosophy was somewhat derivative from *Nicomachoan Ethics* developed by Aristotle. For example, according to Aristotle, the highest pursuit by which to attain happiness is the human's intellectual ability to reason. Thus, humans must seek to excel at the one thing that no other natural being on earth is capable, i.e., living rationally by employing our

---

5. Alter, *Hebrew Bible*, 3:673.
6. Walsh, introduction to *Nature of the Gods*, xiv.

INTRODUCTION

superior intellect. Living rationally through intellect requires the human to deliberate carefully, unemotionally, and intentionally to understand reality concerning which actions to take to maximize happiness. The reality is, virtuous living will result in happiness. The end goal is to live a virtuous complete life. To accomplish this the person must develop habits of moral virtue—taking the right action. It starts with intentionally performing the right action through reason. A single virtuous act does not constitute virtuous living any more than choosing to tell the truth on a single occasion makes a person honest. It is through repetitively preforming virtuous acts that turn into habits that people become virtuous.[7] Cicero, in his dialogue between two characters (Balbus and Cotta) in *Nature of the Gods*, compares virtue in a legalistic fashion with the "*nature of the gods*" to emphasis their action or nonaction in human affairs. The argument here is: no one attributes virtue to God. In antiquity, gods were credited when humans experienced good fortunes—i.e., they must have done something that pleased the gods. Likewise, the gods were also credited when humans experienced bad fortunes—they fail to please the gods by making inadequate sacrifice, etc. However, no one ever praised or thanked the gods for being virtuous. Cicero's point was, the way a person lived had no impact on whether or not that person would experience good or bad fortune. Cicero's primary focus was to understand the nature of the gods pertaining to human affairs. In this dialogue, however, Cicero demonstrated an important element in ancient thought—that humans were solely responsible for their virtuous or non-virtuous acts. Moreover, he introduced a new way to understand divine influences in human affairs. Indeed, a deity's primary role was not to exercise punitive measures on humans who practiced deviant behavior nor was it to issue rewards for good behavior. "The fact is that one's character, and the kind of life which one has lived, has no bearing on one's good or evil fortune."[8] This argument strongly resembles the one found in Qohelet's contention: "Since the same fate comes to all, to the righteous and the wicked, to the good and

---

7. Aristotle, *Nicomachean Ethics*, 23–25, 118–19 (1139b–1140a), 216 (1177a).

8. Cicero, *Nature of the Gods*, 143.

INTRODUCTION

the evil, to the clean and the unclean, to those who sacrifice and to those who do not sacrifice. As are the good, so are the sinners; those who swear are like those who shun an oath. This is an evil in all that happens under the sun, that the same fate comes to everyone" (Eccl 9:2–3). If the deity is not the influencer in human affairs, what passion is responsible for the individual's will to continue participating in their existence—what gives meaning to their life, if behavior does not dictate fate? The first chapter will demonstrate that the linear progression which emerged was a result of Hellenistic philosophy integrated with Christian theology to produce a new mentality held by humanity.

CHAPTER 1

Existentialism

THE WELL-KNOW SLOGAN AMONG existentialists "existence precedes essence" captures the heart of the philosophy. A person can, however, exist without an essence, but the person (according to the philosophy) can choose what their essence will be. Christian theologians argue that the choices a person makes affects their character. However, it is impossible for a person to choose their essence because an essence is a set of properties a thing possesses and if it were to lose any of them, it would cease to exist. If a person can choose their own essence, there must have been a time when the person existed but failed to have an essence. A person can exist but not possess a set of properties required for existence? Impossible! Existentialism, loosely defined, is concerned with finding meaning in the seemingly absurd nature of life and the quest for validation. It is an attempt to produce a meaningful existence prescribed to human life from the position of the individual, rather than from a detached spectator. Existential philosophies vary considerably, depending on whether or not the philosopher believes in God or is an atheist.[1]

Paul Tillich discussed the connection to a person's essence and courage in *The Courage to Be*. Tillich turns to Western thought for this self-affirmation process. "Courage is an ethical reality, but it

---

1. Elwell, *Evangelical Dictionary of Theology*, 424.

is rooted in the whole breadth of human existence and ultimately in the structure of being itself."[2] The Western sources Tillich relied on to explain the connection between courage, virtue, and existentialism begins with stoic ideas and extends into the sociological developments of Platonic thought, Aristotle's preservation of the aristocratic element in courage, and Thomas Aquinas's doctrine of courage. Plato, according to Tillich, recognized an essential function of humanity's essence, an ethical value and sociological quality—the *thymoeides*. Essentially, *thymoeides* was a combination of courage and an element related to the soul, the *thymós*. The *thymós* is between the intellectual and sensual element in humanity, bridging the gap between reason and desire. In conjunction, the *thymoeides* is related to a level of society called the *phylakes* (guardians). The *phylakes* represented the armed aristocracy of all that was graceful and noble; from this comes the bearers of wisdom adding wisdom to courage. However, when the aristocracy and its values disintegrated, they were lost to the ancient world as well as to the modern bourgeoisie. The bearers of enlightened reasoning and technologically organized masses took their place.[3] Nevertheless, the aristocratic element was preserved in Aristotle's philosophy. According to Aristotle, true courage is acting on what is noble. Beasts, for example, are not courageous because they are moved by instinct, fear, and rage. They rush into danger without foreseeing the consequences. Rage may assist in human action, but it requires a combination of deliberate purpose and the right motives for it to be real courage.[4] Courage, therefore, is the affirmation of a person's essence. Moreover, the greatest test of courage is the willingness of a person to sacrifice their life. The soldier, by their very profession, must always be ready to provide this sacrifice. Thus, the definition of courage has morphed into that of the soldier's, as an example. The language pertaining to courage in both the Latin and the Greek indicate a military connection with the word. By the Middle Ages, however, aristocratic values associated with courage were revived and once

2. Tillich, *Courage to Be*, 3.
3. Tillich, *Courage to Be*, 6–7.
4. Aristotle, *Nicomachean Ethics*, 57 (117a).

again courage became characteristic of the nobility. Knights, for example, represented courage—they were simultaneously soldiers and noblemen. During this period there were two concepts of courage: the heroic-aristocratic ethics of the early Middle Ages and the rational-democratic ethics—a "heritage of the Christian-humanistic tradition."[5] Thomas Aquinas expressed these concepts in his doctrine of courage. Aquinas takes a dualistic approach to courage. There is wisdom courage representing the "strength of mind," which is capable of conquering anything that threatens the achievement of the highest good. The second is venturing courage, which participates in the creation of wisdom. Aquinas defends the limited meaning of courage with the example of a soldier's courage and integrates "the aristocratic structure of medieval society with the universalist elements of Christianity and humanism."[6]

Tillich continued his thesis on "the courage to be" utilizing Stoic philosophy by disclosing that courage, for the Stoics, is in the ontological and the moral sense of the definition. They simultaneously had an interdependence of the fear of death and the fear of life along with an interdependence of the courage to live and the courage to die. This parallels with the philosophy in Qohelet, who sees the meaningless and absurdity in life. The enigmatic experiences of life, dealt by fate, create anxieties for the living, and the thought of death adds to their depression; even those who have lost the will to live cannot escape. Suicide, because of fear, contradicts the Stoic's accepted version of courage. Their appeal to suicide represented a person who has conquered life, not a person who has been conquered by life. Qohelet expressed: "All things are wearisome: more than one can express; the eye is not satisfied with seeing, or the ear filled with hearing. What has been is what will be, and whatever has been done is what will be done; there is nothing new under the sun" (Eccl 1:8–9). The Stoics would argue this may be a result of the "pleasure principle"—i.e., the pursuit of excessive pleasure has resulted in a disgusted and disparaging outlook for the individual. Courage for the Stoics was the ability to reason: "The courage to be is to affirm

---

5. Tillich, *Courage to Be*, 8.
6. Tillich, *Courage to Be*, 9.

one's own reasonable nature over and against what is accidental in us."[7] Reason is humanity's essential nature, but anxiety cannot be argued away nor can reason create courage. Reason does, however, allow humanity to distinguish between natural and unnatural desire. Natural desire is limited. However, unnatural desire—humanity's untamed imagination—is unlimited and distorts their ability to obtain satisfaction.[8] Whether or not an individual arrives at an existential crisis due to excessive indulgence is not a primary concern here. It is relevant to the philosophy, but the opposite could just as easily be the result of existential issues. It is vanity on any level that brings into question the meaning of life that must be considered. A poverty-stricken individual, for example, may contemplate the point of their existence. Nevertheless, it's those who are wealthy that typically possess an abundance of idle time allowing their imagination to reach unlimited desires. A good example is provided by the nineteenth-century philosopher and theologian Søren Kierkegaard. In his own personal journal, Kierkegaard recorded that he was living lavishly on his inheritance as a student. He experienced feelings of boredom and futility; he attributed these feelings to his excessive pursuit of pleasure. He became so agitated with his struggle to find meaning and direction in his life, at one point, he considered suicide. Through reason he finds a solution, writing: "What I really need is to come to terms with myself about what I am to do, not about what I am to know, except insomuch as knowledge must precede every act. It is a matter of understanding my destiny, of seeing what the Divinity actually wants me to do; what counts is to find the truth, which is true for me, to find that idea for which I will live and die."[9] This is the traditional fundamental idea behind existential philosophy—each individual is responsible for determining that which gives meaning to their life. That "idea" or purpose becomes the reason for their continued existence and worthy of self-sacrifice—the affirmation of a person's existence.

---

7. Tillich, *Courage to Be*, 14.
8. Tillich, *Courage to Be*, 15.
9. Kierkegaard, *Christianity in Training*, xxiv, para. 2.

Tillich used the ancients' philosophy to emphasize the important role of the individual. In order to come to terms with life's vanity, each individual must engage in the process, i.e., become a participant rather than exist as a detached spectator. It is reason and courage, defined by the ancients, that enables the traditional existentialist to find meaning in their life. For example, reason brings the philosophy to its logical conclusion. True courage is a derivative of this reason existing only in humans, expressed by Aristotle, that enables the individual to participate. The emphasis on courage should not be taken lightly because without courage reasoning cannot satisfy the human condition. Thus, an existentialist is not literally choosing their essence, as mentioned at the beginning of the chapter. The existentialist, through reasoning and courage, is choosing the purpose for which they will live and die; thereby assigning meaning to their life. For example, if a soldier is removed from their occupation and is assigned a job in the civilian sector, the soldier's essence has not changed—their identity does not hinge on their occupation (at least it shouldn't). The person's occupation (soldier in this case) may give meaning to their life, but the essence of who they are still exists even when their occupation changes. Although, the individual must now find a new meaning for their life.

SPECULATIVE AND ANALYTICAL PHILOSOPHY OF HISTORY

There is a distinction between secular and Christian philosophy pertaining to existentialism which assigns value to the human condition as a whole depending on how the discipline of history is approached. Speculative philosophy of history attempts to construct an all-encompassing history—a universal history that accounts for the rise and decline of empires, states, and cultures. Modern historians have substituted the practice of connecting major events to the unfolding of history on a grand scale, for narrowly focused specialist studies. "History proper," as noted by scholar M. C. Lemon, has mostly been phased out and replaced with controversial contemporary social studies ranging from a number of ideological concerns.[10] Speculative philosophy of history is concerned with analyzing the content of history as a whole to extract a meaningful account of the past. It takes into account the various mentalities over the ages and contemplates what mechanism controls the course of human history, i.e., does Fate or Providence have a role? The emergence of modern science and social studies, at least in the contemporary sense, have discounted this philosophical approach to history.[11] Analytic philosophy of history critically examines the thought process historians apply to their discipline. They critique the historian's methods for obtaining information related to the past and question whether or not the narrative results in historical knowledge. Philosophy of history is concerned with both of these branches, speculative and analytic. The speculative treats history as a large unfolding of human affairs in the past. Thereby, it searches for meaningful connections by approaching history as an "object." As mentioned, analytic philosophy of history treats history as an academic discipline by critiquing the speculative approach. In other words, the analytic branch studies history "for its own sake," collecting facts and reporting events; it is not concerned with assigning meaning to the past.[12] A defense for speculative philosophy of history was perhaps best expressed by M. C. Lemon:

> Broadly, its project is interesting in its own right since it purports to "make sense" of history, and to that extent suggests answers to the meaning of life . . . And in an increasingly secular age where religion is less appealed to for answers to that question, speculative philosophy of history is all we have left . . . for those who dismiss the question of "the meaning of life" on the a priori grounds that there simply isn't one, perhaps the burden of proof is on them to show, from history, its meaningless.[13]

Whatever argument can be made regarding approaches to studying history, Lemon's notation that religion is becoming less

10. Lemon, *Philosophy of History*, 1–2.
11. Lemon, *Philosophy of History*, 8–9.
12. Lemon, *Philosophy of History*, 7–8, 281, para. 3.
13. Lemon, *Philosophy of History*, 12.

useful for the modern age when it comes to answering existential questions, that is, questions associated with the meaning of life, is factual. However, that trend has not prevented the εκλεκτός "elect" orthodox Christians from keeping with the tradition of viewing history as linear, as opposed to a cyclical view of history.

Cyclical versus Linear Understanding of Time

The ancients understood the past different than modern historians, evident in their writings. They had a mythical view of space and time. They believed there was an eternal reoccurring cycles of events in history. The ancients were void of any idea of progress for humanity in this eternal wheel of fate. They told their history through mythical stories, that should not be confused with fables. Fables were the work of fantasies that no one was expected to believe. Unlike fables, ancient myths had a semblance of truth. Often these stories were regarded as divine or sacred and had relevant applications for their societies. Debates have emerged on whether these ancient stories, told by their authors, were meant to be understood as allegorical or factual. This, however, is a strictly modern view of ancient narratives. The ancients did not view the world the same as from a modern's perspective. Moderns attempt to understand the world through observation and rational thought. The world, from a modern's perspective, is detached and can be objectively scrutinized. Unlike the modern's perspective, the ancients did not view the world as distinct or separate from themselves. Their world was animated—alive, willful, calculated. For the ancients, floods, plagues, and various other naturally occurring phenomenon were understood as the results of actions taken by this animated world surrounding them. Interpreting nature this way resulted in directly experiencing it. Thus, being part of the animated world connected them to an intellectual mediation for epistemological developments, i.e., processes for knowing. The debate over whether the ancients believed their myths to be true is derived from an inaccurate perspective.[14] Lemon argued that "they lived their daily

14. Lemon, *Philosophy of History*, 16–17.

lives within a mythical consciousness in the first place."[15] Perhaps it should be understood that mythical stories from the ancients are more practical than factual—they succeeded in making sense of their experiences. Whether or not all elements of their stories are true is beside the point. For example, in the future our present way of knowing may be superseded by a development that is unfathomable to our current thought process.[16] Whatever false mentalities are held in the current age regarding our understanding of the world, they should not be condemned from the advantage point of future generations. For the same reason we cannot discredit the value of the ancients' understanding of their world. The ancients falsely believed that the sun orbited the earth but were still able to make accurate calculations regarding seasonal and celestial events (summer/winter solstice, eclipses).

The notion of causation, i.e., the operation of impersonal laws governing events were absent in the ancients' view. They made no real attempt to understand events. Mainly, because it was irrelevant to them. Often, they would credit the gods for various underlying factors that occurred in their animated world. Moreover, there was no concept of humanity's progress. Thus, time, for the ancients, would go around in this vast historical cycle void of meaning.[17] There was a cycle of regularities—daily, monthly, yearly events that would all return to the point where they began. Flood, draught, and famine were inevitably repetitive. They concluded that if nature went in circles, so did humanity.[18] Nothing of real value could be expected from the physical world, so they looked to the afterlife as something of value to be cherished.[19] Around 500 BC there is a shift in mentality expressed by Hellenistic culture.[20] Many retained the

---

15. Lemon, *Philosophy of History*, 17.
16. Lemon, *Philosophy of History*, 19.
17. Lemon, *Philosophy of History*, 22.
18. Lemon, *Philosophy of History*, 32.
19. Lemon, *Philosophy of History*, 24.
20. Lemon, *Philosophy of History*, 29, para. 3.

circular understanding of time. However, there was a shift from the mythical understanding to the philosophical.[21]

The passing of time is an important concept for the Christian that understands existentialist views. The Christian religion has strong connections to the writings and prophecies of the Old Testament. The authors of the Old Testament viewed their world in much the same way as other ancient Near Eastern cultures. Moreover, scholars have noted the parallels between the mythical stories of the Near East and those of the Old Testament. Some scholars claim that the Hebrews took the stories from their ancient Near Eastern predecessors and "sanitized" them by removing mythical elements related to magic and polytheistic deities. A polemical theory was developed by Christian scholars which is used to counter pagan myths. For example, the Canaanite storm-god Baal is depicted, in Ugaritic literature, as "riding on the clouds." Ugaritic literature pre-dates Hebrew writings.[22] The book of Isaiah, therefore, is criticizing Baalism when Yahweh is depicted as riding on a cloud. "Baal does not ride on clouds; Yahweh does!"[23] Ancient Hebrew writings, however, reveal a distinctive thought process pertaining to human origins and the passing of time. While many of these parallels could not have happened by mere chance, there are some important dissimilarities. For example: all societies of the Near East were polytheist, except Hebrew; the gods of Near Eastern culture had limits, i.e., they were not omnipotent; the Hebrew's God is depicted as transcendent—he is not part of his creation, but he rules it; and most importantly, humanity was created in God's image, the exact opposite of ancient Near Eastern deities.[24] It was the Hebrew's mentality regarding the origins of the cosmos and Yahweh's purposely driven agenda, through his mediation with Abraham, that laid the foundations for a linear view of history held by the Christians.

Judeo-Christian monotheism and their understanding of time had implications for developments of existential philosophy

---

21. Lemon, *Philosophy of History*, 29, para. 3.
22. Currid, *Against the Gods*, 28.
23. Currid, *Against the Gods*, 28, para. 2.
24. Currid, *Against the Gods*, 40, para. 3.

by rejecting the idea of cosmic and historical cycles of reoccurrences. In the Christian's view, God had created the cosmos—it had a beginning and it was finite, according to God's plan for humanity. Therefore, history is linear. Although the Greeks and Romans had shifted toward a mentality of logic and reason (philosophy), their views of history mostly remained endlessly repeatable without purpose. Emphasis is placed on "mostly" because the secular contributions to the meaning of life should not been dismissed. Specifically, as previously demonstrated, the philosophy of Aristotle. He provided good reason for an individual's purpose, i.e., to live a virtuous life. It was, according to *Nicomachean Ethics*, in the best interest of the individual to live virtuously. However, it was Christian thinkers who applied these principles to humanity on a grand scale. They integrated the philosophy with their theology and connected it to human history, which provided humanity with a meaningful past. For most of the Greco-Roman world the accomplishments that distinguished cultures and societies were irrelevant. This is because nothing of significance could transcend humanity into a progressive future since they were entrapped in a circle of cosmic repetition. Essentially, there was no meaning or purpose to history because they lacked the concept of progress as a whole for the human race. For the Christians, however, history was always unique. The transcending guidance through time and history of a deliberate God enables humanity to look forward with confidence that his will is being fulfilled. Whatever disasters may occur, however puzzling the future may seem, the history of humanity is not dismissed as an infinite cycle of unintelligent natural events, but an intentional plan developed by a rational supreme mind.[25]

---

25. Lemon, *Philosophy of History*, 56.

Chapter 2

Distorted Courage, the Great Regression, and Morality

FRIEDRICH NIETZSCHE WAS BORN on October 15, 1844. His father was a Lutheran pastor who died when Nietzsche was four years old. His mother, Franziska, raised him and his sister, Elisabeth. Nietzsche attended the most prestigious boarding school in Germany. Before studying classical philology at the University of Leipzig, he spent a year studying theology at the University of Bonn. Nietzsche, despite being in poor health, managed to publish a book every year from 1878 to 1887.[1] Occasionally, the comments made in his writing seem to loosen the structure of his position in the overall narrative. Thus, there are variations in the interpretations of the philosophy by his audience. This could be, however, attributed to his editor who was also his sister—Elisabeth. Elisabeth, with the help of coconspirators, edited and published Nietzsche's work to support their political agenda.[2] This was done either after Nietzsche's death or when he was incoherent after suffering a collapse in 1889, while walking the streets of Turin, Italy. For the next eleven years he was under the care of his family.[3] Nietzsche's most recent work includes *The Antichrist*

---

1. Nietzsche, *Antichrist*, viii.
2. Nietzsche, *Antichrist*, Intro., xv, para. 2.
3. Nietzsche, *Antichrist*, Intro., ix.

(1895). *The Antichrist* is considered the most extreme criticism against modern values and beliefs. It was directed at the Christian church and their belief system. Some modern philosophers defend Nietzsche's critique of Christianity as being directed exclusively at the institution, the church. However, there are many instances where Nietzsche seemed to specifically address the individual who practices Christianity.

Nietzsche had such contempt for humanity that he boasted of his deceptive philosophy. A philosophy which advocated for a distorted version of courage. This "forbidden courage" Nietzsche propagated is not courage in any sense of the definition defined by Aristotle and embraced by the Christian theologians. Nietzsche relied on basic psychological rhetoric to prime his audience. Perhaps he intended to give them the illusion that they were literary elitists, by suggesting that few would comprehend his profound philosophy. In the preface of *The Antichrist*, he begins with the statement: "This book is for the very few." He goes on to express that perhaps only future generations will be enlightened enough to comprehend the profoundness of his ideas. Describing the person with the capacity for such understanding he continues: "He must be intellectually upright . . . He must be used to living on mountain tops . . . Such men alone are my readers, my proper readers, my preordained readers: of what account are the rest?"[4] Humility is an attribute perhaps too Christian for Nietzsche to embrace. Nietzsche's argument is that Christianity is in conflict with humanity's instinct—that which makes humanity valuable, i.e., humanity's strength or the "will to power."[5] He explained this using Darwinian characteristics with the contention that it is pity that makes a person defective. Christianity, according to Nietzsche, has diminished the individual's will and even corrupted the person's intellect by presenting the strong person as the typical villain.[6] For Nietzsche, it was not original sin, as the Christians had claimed, that distorted humanity's reason, but Christianity itself.

4. Nietzsche, preface to *Antichrist*, xxiii.
5. Nietzsche, *Antichrist*, 4.
6. Nietzsche, *Antichrist*, 5.

Distorted Courage, the Great Regression, and Morality

There is a stark contrast between Nietzsche and Aristotle regarding courage and reason. Nietzsche insisted that humanity's greatest, most trusted characteristic is instinct. However, unlike the beast, this animal man has stifled his evolutionary destiny and became the most botched and diseased of the animals because humanity has wandered furthest from their instincts.[7] If we recall from the previous chapter, true courage, according to Aristotle, is acting on what is noble. Beasts act upon their primal instinct devoid of any concept of nobility or virtue. Therefore, beasts are not courageous because they are moved by simple instinct, i.e., fear and rage. Their instinct drives them to rush into danger without foreseeing the consequences. Unlike the beast that is driven by instinct, humans can display the greatest test of courage through the willingness of self-sacrifice. Humans have the ability, that courage provides, to reasonably place value on the human condition and determine that for which they are willing to live and die. It's apparent that Nietzsche failed to confront this problem. Advocating for humanity to embrace their primal instincts denies the civil course humanity has been mostly able to sustain. If nobility, virtue, or pity—the most undesirable traits of humanity, according to Nietzsche, are repressed the human race reduces itself to the same level as beasts. Nietzsche's thinking was likely compromised by his disdain for Christianity. His general critique of religion, however, has some validity. Specifically, when he notes that "the best way of leading mankind by the nose is with morality!"[8]

Clearly, Nietzsche's accusations regarding the institution's exploitation of humanity during certain episodes throughout history has merit. However, to charge the essence of the theology as being flawed is naive or malicious. As demonstrated, Christian theology integrated with specified revelations from antiquity, that is, logic, reason, and courage are values that apply to the existential problem. These attributes connected to the human condition produced meaning and purpose beyond that of the individual. These attributes are pertinent to history on a grand scale, removing humanity

---

7. Nietzsche, *Antichrist*, 12.
8. Nietzsche, *Antichrist*, 47.

from the monotonous cycle of fate. It was the revelation of progress that enabled philosophers and theologians to correctly understand history as linear. Nevertheless, Nietzsche insisted on pushing humanity toward a great regression. He argued that we must embrace nihilism—there is no truth, everything is meaningless, and humanity is indeed on a repetitive cycle. Western values must be rejected and replaced with a device of each person's own creation. These implications have proven to be detrimental for modern contemporary societies. The highest values held in social justice movements (critical race theory) are derivatives from Nietzsche's philosophy. Guilt, for example, is the antidote to long-held practical Western values. This does not suggest that Nietzsche's ideas are synonymous with the ancients' worldview. Nietzsche's ideas, however, are monotones of the same mentality.

Providence and Patterns in History

Patterns and regularities do occur throughout history. This confirmation does not, by any stretch, discredit the linear theory of history. The Italian philosopher Giambattista Vico best illustrated this in his publication titled *New Science*. Vico noticed patterns and regularities existing in all societies throughout history where civilizations rise, peak, and collapse. For many, once the revelation of humanity's progression was accepted, cyclical fatalism was no longer a viable historical theory. Moreover, the idea of fate, pertaining to history, whether it be cyclical or linear, is not the primary concern of advocates who see history through the lens of providence. Providence does not decree the collapse of each period in history. It is flawed human nature manifested in free will which sets societies on the path to destruction.[9] If not for providence, free will combined with an unlimited imagination would prevent the progress of societies. This is evident in a society's ability to reorganize and avoid destructive paths. Providence, which must be an extension from an eternal source, is a built-in feature at work within society. It works within the metaphysical realms of

---

9. Lemon, *Philosophy of History*, 160.

the human psyche by administrating demonstrative pressures of persuasion. In other words, it works with humanity's conscience attempting to deliver the best outcomes without a complete transgression on their sovereignty. Occasionally, however, there are times when the eternal source of providence intervenes irrespective of human desire or intention. This idea of providence is not empirically based, i.e., it is impossible to prove or debunk. From a philosophical position the patterns and regularities existing in history coincide with the theoretical understanding of a linear philosophy of history. Nevertheless, providence does not guarantee the continuation of a civilization. On a quantitative scale, the struggle for each individual's mind within society pertaining to their ability to exercise free will while controlling their passions not only determines a civilization's course in history, it is the deciding factor for their continued existence. Therefore, since the future of a nation is determined by the population's aggregated moral behavior, each individual has the obligation to practice virtue and self-discipline.

The idea of a civilization's survival being directly proportional to their morality was not exclusive to Christian theology. *Nicomachean Ethics* suggests that deviant behavior is not only destructive to the recipients (victims), it is just as destructive for the person engaging in undesirable actions. Moreover, the Roman Empire credited their success to their ability to sustain discipline—both on and off the battlefield. Other Roman writers notice a decline in superiority as societal shifts occurred. Livy, for example, attributed Rome's corruption to their Greek adopted life style, i.e., luxuries living and a lax in morality.[10] The warnings present in certain works of antiquity (Greek and Roman) regarding morality fell mostly on deaf ears—both of these great civilizations collapsed. Vico would have argued this was providence at work—not that providence was responsible for the collapse of these great civilizations (essentially it was moral decadence exemplified by the majority in the population) but providence provided foundational knowledge for political systems to improve upon in

---

10 Spawforth, *Greece and the Augustan Cultural Revolution*, 14–15.

the future. Perhaps the best example is the United States—evident in their system of government. Nonetheless, in the range of eighteen hundred years and well acquainted with ancient history, these documented events did not prevent Nietzsche from idealizing humanity's basic instincts.

Origins of Morality

As the philosophy of existentialism comes into focus, it should be evident that morality is foundational to existential issues pertaining to the human condition. The objectifiable source responsible for humanity's morality has been imprinted on their souls. According to Thomas Aquinas, humans are the only creatures made in the image of God who are both intelligent and spiritual, with the capacity to know God and receive his wisdom. Humanity's morality and motives for seeking justice, therefore, are the by-product of God's creation that originated when humans were created in God's image. Original sin nearly destroyed the image of God in humanity, resulting in the depravity of intellect and the bondage of will. However, God's image was not completely removed from them. The evidence for this extends from a universal tendency found in every culture regardless of time or place—humans have believed in the existence of a higher reality—a greater force that exceeds the human race collectively. Moreover, the intellectual life focuses on reason and will, leading to a shift in the image of God in man. The relation between intelligence that allows for the capacity of speech and the development of ideas unite reason with will to produce free will. Thereby, placing the image of God in the power of humans to act responsibly on a moral level. For example, free will, according to Aquinas, is progressively formed in humans to produce moral acts consistent with the image of God. The freedom developed in this process is imperfect, that is, free will agents can still sin, but as the process continues and humans make an effort to conform to the image of God, the stronger the will becomes to deny sinful

DISTORTED COURAGE, THE GREAT REGRESSION, AND MORALITY

acts.[11] Thus, humans have the capacity to make ethical choices that correspond to the image of God.

In the modern age, however, the image of God within humanity is often distorted, suppressed, and even denied by the *intelligentsia*. *Intelligentsia* is a word of Latin origin describing intellectuals who desire power in order to engineer society into their utopian version of how the world should be. The *intelligentsia* first appeared in Europe during the sixteenth century. Most were lay thinkers approaching philosophical questions through the lens of progressive science rather than theology or the church, which was previously the tradition. The advancements in science suggested to many that the only entities that existed were those that could be measured and observed—in contrast to religion and the church that rely on metaphysical claims and the belief that each individual possess a soul. The idea of progressive science was irresistible to intellectuals as they began to see themselves as the ancient Greek and Roman philosophers whose job it was to intervene in the lives of citizens. While ordinary citizens pursued a living, the intellectuals were the only ones with the capacity to engineer the science of human affairs. They dismissed disciplines such as economics and political theory, viewing them as irrelevant due to being formed as a result of trial and error. They swayed public opinion and many intellectuals became politicians, free to pursue their private ambitions in the guise of working for the common good. Historian Richard Pipes describes the *intelligentsia's* ideology as materialistic—regarding humans not as unique individuals with immortal souls, but as exclusively physical entities produced by their environment. This justifies their desire to engineer "a new breed of perfectly virtuous creatures" through the restructuring of society.[12] The working theory introduced in this analysis is: once social unrest begins to develop in a society, the seeds of discontent among the population will take root only if they are followed by a multiplier effect (a propaganda campaign launched by the agitators) which is exasperated by a serious of

---

11. Pinckaers et al., "Ethics and the Image of God," 34, 37–38.
12. Pipes, *Concise History of the Russian Revolution*, 21, 31.

systematic global interruptions. The *intelligentsia*, with the help of outside influencers, will capitalize on the crisis until a revolutionary change in society occurs. In the process, however, the *intelligentsia* has discarded all eternal truths providence has provided for a civilization's well-being.

For a God-fearing society, however, there still exists an internal sense of deity that is continuously present and functioning in the human experience. Moreover, for the psalmist, there exists a universal language providing constant evidence of the greatness of this deity evident in nature.[13] "The heavens declare the glory of God; the skies proclaim the work of his hands" (Ps 19:1). The claim that this moral code which dwells in humanity and installed at Creation, is evident in Scripture when God said, "Let us make man in our image, in our likeness . . . So God created man in his own image, in the image of God" (Gen 1:26–27); and when he told Israel, "I am the Lord your God; consecrate yourselves and be holy, because I am holy. Do not make yourselves unclean by any creature that moves about the ground. I am the Lord who brought you up out of Egypt to be your God; therefore, be holy, because I am holy" (Lev 11:44–45).[14] Thus, moral obligations must be understood in terms of their connection to God's requirements for his creation. The Cappadocian Fathers, when referring to the image of God and morality, support the idea of God as being the standard for evaluating morality in societies. Regarding creation and man as God's image bearer, Gregory of Nyssa argued, "Neither the heavens nor the moon nor the sun nor the beauty of the stars nor any of the other phenomena of creation," could claim the title given to man in Genesis, "image of God."[15] Gregory of Nazianzus directed the following at government officials: "You are the image of God, and you rule over those who are the image of God!"[16] He made it clear that the doctrine of the image of God was key to

---

13. Schreiner, *King in His Beauty*, 5–6.
14. Erickson, *Christian Theology*, 257.
15. Pelikan, "Image of God," 123.
16. Pelikan, "Image of God," 123, para. 2.

societal ethics.[17] Something which cannot be inferred in secular philosophy regarding morality, articulated by C. Stephen Evans is: "A God who provides the basis for moral obligations must be understood as a moral being, a being who cares deeply about the realization of moral values."[18]

17. Pelikan, "Image of God," 124.
18. Evans and Manis, *Philosophy of Religion*, 96.

CHAPTER 3

Historical Context and Background

THE DATE OF THE composition for the book of Ecclesiastes is highly contested and the ranges vary considerably. The dating is not a primary concern for this work beyond casting doubt on claims that Hellenistic sources influenced the philosophy of this Old Testament author. Nevertheless, the Greek language had an impact on late Jewish communities, but only in terms of their ability to communicate their already established writings. The Septuagint, for example, uses the Greek version εκκλησιαστής from the Greek root εκκλησία, meaning: assembly, gathering, summoned legislative body, church.[1] This Greek word is substituted for the Hebrew word קֹהֶלֶת (Qohelet). The Greek word εκκλησιαστής translates phonetically into English as Ecclesiastes, the title of the book. There are a few instances where the ending of the Hebrew word indicate it may represent a vocation. In one occurrence, it is preceded by the definite article suggesting it is a title. Some English translations use the word "teacher" or "preacher." Thus, because of these discrepancies, i.e., inability to prove the identity of original author, many scholars have chosen to use the untranslated Hebrew word—Qohelet.[2]

The book of Ecclesiastes is typically assigned to wisdom literature. Certain books in this genre clearly demonstrate that a person's

---

1. Danker, *Greek-English Lexicon*, 303, def. 1.
2. Alter, *Hebrew Bible*, 673.

character has no impact on their good or bad fortune in life. Job's circumstances, for example, portrayed an instance where the innocent suffer. That same mentality is confirmed here by Qohelet. According to Qohelet, God's disposition is unknowable. Apparently, there exists a decree that God has withheld from humanity. Some scholars claim there is a conflict among wisdom literature. Proverbs, for example, seems to affirm that the fear of God guarantees long life and prosperity.[3] Perhaps an argument could be made that these statements found in Proverbs are value statements and not promises or guarantees. Moreover, the eternal or metaphysical aspect is often overlooked and assumptions are made pertaining to the immediate physical well-being of an individual.

Qohelet is unique; unlike Mesopotamian wisdom, he does not attempt to predict events by observing signs. Even cycles in nature are unpredictable, other than the fact that they will reoccur—when and how remain uncertain. Unlike Job, he refused to address God, instead he complained to his own heart.[4] He rejects the notion that there exists any pattern or preference of victims chosen by death. Some scholars have advocated for a disturbing narrative in Qohelet's philosophy. They argue that Qohelet is demonstrating that there is no distinction between the beasts and humans—both will die. Further, there is no comfort from the thought of them returning to their source.[5] It is true that the same sovereign deity that gives life may also recall it and humans have limited power to correct inequalities. It is for these reasons Qohelet declared an avenue that is essential for individuals to pursue. He recognized that in the absence of an eternal and objectifiable source, death destroys all of humanity's advancements. The ability to reason at this level distinguishes humans from beasts. It is the reality of this problem that leads to paralysis for many individuals. For those who do not recognize an eternal objectifiable source, human life is just as meaningless as the life of beasts. Consumed with fear, death has

---

3. Crenshaw, *Ecclesiastes*, 23.
4. Crenshaw, *Ecclesiastes*, 24.
5. Crenshaw, *Ecclesiastes*, 24, para. 5.

a grip on the unreasonable long before they die.[6] Nearing the end of the book, Qohelet promoted "the fear of the Lord." He distinguished between those who fear God and the evildoers who do not fear God. Fearing God was not about extending one's life—he made this clear "though sinners do evil a hundred times and prolong their lives. . ." (Eccl 8:12). This passage was concerning divine judgment after life on earth. This work will not argue against the prevailing theory concerning Near Eastern beliefs pertaining to the netherworld or Sheol. It is presumed, however, that Enoch was presented with an alternative to Sheol, leaving the possibility open. Nonetheless, in his final statement, Qohelet expressed the importance of fearing God. "Fear God, and keep his commandments; for this is the whole duty of everyone" (Eccl 12:13). The passage in 8:12 supports the argument and does not solely depend on whether the last verses of the final chapter are accepted as original or the work of an editor. Furthermore, Qohelet's existential philosophy, which advocates for pursuing pleasure in certain activities, contains this key element (the fear of the Lord) in other books of wisdom literature.

The Fear of the Lord

The phrase "the fear of the Lord" is central to the book of Proverbs. It calls for a reverence and obedience to God that will foster virtuous behavior. Moreover, the phrase is part of a statement that is exclusive to Israelite writings, not prevalent in the Wisdom texts of Egypt or Mesopotamia.[7] The English word "fear" was derived from the Hebrew word יִרְאַת (yir'ah). Meaning: to fear, to reverence.[8] The English word "Lord" was derived from the Hebrew word יְהוָה (yeh-ho-vaw), Meaning: "Jehovah, pr. name of the supreme God amongst the Hebrew."[9] The phrase is used three times in the first two chapters of Proverbs. It is found in the following verses: Proverbs 1:7, occurring in a positive setting corresponding to

6. Crenshaw, *Ecclesiastes*, 25.
7. Alter, *Hebrew Bible*, 354.
8. Blue Letter Bible, "yir'ah—Gesenius' Hebrew-Chaldee Lexicon."
9. Blue Letter Bible, "Yehovah—Gesenius' Hebrew-Chaldee Lexicon."

knowledge—a statement. Proverbs 1:29, occurring in a negative setting corresponding to knowledge—the result of not choosing to fear the Lord. Proverbs 2:5, in a positive setting corresponding to knowledge, but beyond the simple statement made in Proverbs 1:7. In Proverbs 2:5, the author provided more detail related to the phrase; explaining when the student would "understand the fear of the Lord." This is evident in the previous four verses, that is, understanding comes through commitment, obedience, requests, and seeking (Prov 2:1–4).

Francis Brown, R. Driver, and Charles Briggs's Hebrew-English Lexicon (BDB) records several English words for יִרְאָה n.f. fear: great fear, terror, fear of God, reverence, piety. Related to this phrase they have Proverbs 1:29 cross referenced with Isaiah 11:2, Psalm 111:10, Proverbs 9:10, Proverbs 1:7, 15:33, 8:13, and 16:6, "the knowledge (of God) is the beginning of wisdom, and knowledge, the instruction of wisdom is to hate evil, and it involves departing from evil."[10] For the word יהוה, i.e., יְהוָה, BDB records it as "Yahweh, the proper name of the God of Israel." Moreover, according to BDB, "the pronunciation Jehovah was unknown until 1520, when it was introduced by Galatinus; but it was contested by Le Mercier, J. Drusius, and L. Capellus, as against grammatical and historical propriety."[11] Semantic circumstances can be beneficial to understand the meaning of a passage. The following consists of two grouping examples used in English to convey the circumstance: *Cause*, or the reason for the result. The context applies to the phrase in the first two chapters. The cause of, or the beginning of knowledge is "the fear of the Lord." *Contingency*, or the condition. This applies specifically to Proverbs 1:29. "Because they hated knowledge and did not choose the fear of the Lord." The structure of this passage is in a prepositional phrase. It is contingent on fearing the Lord. Because of their choice, not to fear the Lord, when they called upon the wise council, they were not answered.[12]

---

10. Brown et al., *Brown-Driver-Briggs*, 432, ref. 3374.
11. Brown et al., *Brown-Driver-Briggs*, 218, ref. 3068–69.
12. Long, *Grammatical Concepts 101*, 170–71.

Proverbs were used by the ancients to get their point across. The context in which the proverb was spoken must be considered for it to be useful. These proverbs represent true perspectives. The modern reader should note that seeking to understand "the fear of the Lord" through study, obedience, and living virtuously does not guarantee a long, prosperous life. For example, "keep my commandments and you will live" (Prov 7:2) is a value statement expressed in the biblical world, not a promise.[13] There is value in the proverbial phrase "the fear of the Lord is the beginning of knowledge" (Prov 1:7). However, having reverence for God and seeking him does not promise knowledge. The value resides in the application, that is, fearing God. It puts the human condition into perspective by disclosing there is a universal order that humanity can abide in, but it is reserved for those who recognize the divine authority responsible for ordering the universe. This teaching is stressed and summed up in the book of Proverbs several times through the phrase "the fear of the Lord."

The context of the passage in Proverbs 1:7 is a conclusion to the previous verses' authoritative warning on righteous, justice, and understanding. For example, learning, understanding, and gaining instruction through hearing the words of the wise will motivate the student to have reverence for God. Reverence for God is the beginning of knowledge, a concept that the foolish despise. The results of those who fail to fear the Lord are made known in Proverbs 1:29. Those who do not fear God ignored the council of the wise, but when disaster strikes, they seek the instruction of the wise. However, it is too late, they are left at the mercy of their own destructive devices. "Because they hated knowledge and did not choose the fear of the Lord" (Prov 1:29).

The characteristics of someone who has the "fear of the Lord" is revealed throughout the book. Proverbs 2:5 describes someone who has begun to understand the fear of the Lord. As previously mentioned, the preceding four verses exemplify these characteristics. "My child, if you accept my words and treasure up my commandments within you, making your ear attentive to wisdom and

---

13. Walton et al., *IVP Bible Background Commentary*, 561, 564.

inclining your heart to understanding; if you indeed cry out for insight, and raise your voice for understanding; if you seek it like silver, and search for it as for hidden treasures—then you will understand the fear of the Lord and find the knowledge of God" (Prov 2:1–5). From this passage it is evident that the characteristics of this person will be: faithful/obedient, "if you accept my words and treasure up my commandments within you"; sincerity in learning, "if you indeed cry out" and "search for it as for hidden treasures"; and committed to understanding, "making your ear attentive to wisdom and inclining your heart to understanding." The "fear of the Lord," therefore, is not an emotion of terror that accompanies stress and anxiety from a subject who dreads punishment. The phrase exemplifies true reverence for God and humility. The value in the phrase begins to materialize when humanity seeks to understand this order in the universe. This is the context in which Qohelet used the term "fear God" (Eccl 12:13). In other words, life has meaning concealed from humanity's knowledge (Eccl 11:5). However, only God knows this secret decree. Therefore, enjoy your life by finding pleasure in your work and embrace those you love because these things do not exist in Sheol (the grave). Further, since your life is mere breath (short) and you will be held responsible for your deeds in God's judgment, "banish anxiety from your mind" and have reverence for God (Eccl 11:10, 12:1). Perhaps it can be interpreted, from these passages, that individuals whose circumstances are favorable in life but fail to enjoy their life, will be held accountable before God. "Rejoice, young man, while you are young, and let your heart cheer in the days of your youth. Follow the inclinations of your heart and the desire of your eyes, but know for all these things God will bring you into judgment" (Eccl 11:9–10). It's likely that the author of this book would have been in a position to enjoy much pleasure in life. Moreover, he appears to conclude there is an obligation to enjoy life, but not as a hedonist. Qohelet seems to recognize a fault in hedonists' philosophy. Similar to the stoics, who argued that the pursuit of excessive pleasure would result in a disgusted and disparaging outlook for the individual, Qohelet went a step future. He provided a warning for those who pursued their desires. There was the possibility that unrestrained imaginations would result in greater consequences than a disparaging life on earth. In short, the pursuit of desires motivated by humanity's unlimited imagination has eternal consequences. The ancient writers mentioned in this analysis had much in common regarding the deity. Cicero and Qohelet both recognized, essentially, the righteous and the wicked experienced good and bad fortunes with no apparent connection between their actions or character. However, Qohelet is the only one to mention God's judgment. In the absence of an eternal and objectifiable source it is impossible for justice to exist on any level. For example, if the wicked are allowed long and prosperous lives on earth and nothing exists beyond the grave, neither does justice. If the righteous are slaughtered by the wicked and are lost to the abyss, so is justice. Life, therefore, is meaningless and the human race consists of nothing more than a cluster of subjective abominations susceptible to a miserable existence, a slow descent into madness, "a chasing after the wind."

Considering the human condition from the ancients to the modern era, the methods used to understand the world during each of these episodes throughout history—superstition, philosophy, religion, and finally science, which has (for the most part) supplanted each of its predecessors, there is a considerable probability for a more efficient methodological hypothesis to emerge resulting in a completely different way of analyzing phenomena that the current generation cannot comprehend. If so, once this method takes root and becomes the standard practice for a millennium, future generations will look back in dismay at the mentality of the scientific era. It's interesting, however, that through each transitional episode, the idea of a higher authority that surpasses the human condition managed to become embedded within the human psyche. Considering such, it's not surprising that Qohelet (during the early episodes of history) in all his irritation contemplating fate, death, and the vanity of life, would return to this idea in the final passages of the book. It was never the intention of this research to advocate for God's existence. The goal was to reveal the difficulty in assigning meaning to life without an eternal objectifiable source. This is precisely what contributes to the inefficiencies in the philosophy of secular externalism—there is no justice because nothing exists to hold betrayers

Historical Context and Background

of humanity accountable when they manage to evade justice on earth. Thus, humanity is trapped in an equivocal cycle of reoccurrences with no destination. The meaning that secular existentialism attempts to create for humanity has no value. They must commit to a Darwinian mentality similar to the hedonist's position, i.e., maximizing pleasure—even at the expense of others. Members of society turn against each other and the aggregated population begins their decent into decadence.

Date and Influence of the Text

There are several avenues that scholars have pursued attempting to date the text of Qohelet, some have argued that the text was influenced by Hellenistic thought. Thereby, assigning a much later date than what is suggested by the author himself, e.g., "The words of the Teacher, the son of David, king in Jerusalem" in Eccl 1:1 suggest he is Solomon. Many scholars argue that the work could not have been produced by Solomon. Based on various textual analysis the prevailing consensus for the date is sometime during the late Persian and early Hellenistic periods, much later than Solomon's time. It should be noted, however, that the text contained no Greek words in the original Hebrew, which has led some to date the text prior to the conquest of the Levant by Alexander the Great. Still, others argue that the author was influenced by Greek philosophical thought, evident throughout the text.[14] It is precisely this subjective approach, pertaining to Greek philosophy, that this research finds wanting. There are no references to historical events in Qohelet that would constitute as evidence associated with late Persian or early Hellenistic periods.[15] There are, however, economic and cultural shifts some scholars associate with these periods. These connections tend to be subjective—short of any real substance for dating the text. The earliest manuscript of Qohelet stems from a fragment of the Dead Sea Scrolls, approximately 175 BC (4QQoh a).[16] How-

14. *New Oxford Annotated Bible*, 945.
15. *New Oxford Annotated Bible*, 945.
16. *New Oxford Annotated Bible*, 945.

ever, this fragment is a copy. There are no extant manuscripts of the complete Hebrew Bible. It was Jewish custom to destroy older copies of the manuscripts, "so as not to profane them and the name of the Lord."[17] Moreover, in its origins, Hebrew was exclusively consonantal, i.e., without any vowel letters. To clarify pronunciations, over time, Jewish scholars developed a vowel system—making notes around the consonantal text which evolved into a vowel pointing system. The group of Jewish scholars who developed these notes are known as Masoretes. Essentially, they applied vowels to the text without (supposedly) changing the text or its meaning. By the tenth century AD their work became the standard Hebrew Bible, known today as the Masoretic text.[18]

Some scholars have hypothesized that Qohelet was originally written in standard Phoenician orthography (without vowel letters).[19] The Phoenician writing system, a continuation of the Proto-Canaanite system, is the ancestor of Hebrew.[20] Hebrew script has persisted for more than three thousand years.[21] The Babylonian exile marked the disappearance of the language from common use. Before the exile, in 587 BC, the Hebrew script used in the prose sections of the Pentateuch, Prophets, and Writings is known as Classical Biblical Hebrew. Late Biblical Hebrew refers to the sections written after the exile. Biblical Hebrew has survived "artificially" in the Dead Sea Scrolls.[22] Of course, Qohelet is located in the Writings portion of the Hebrew Bible. Nevertheless, as previously mentioned, most scholars do not accept Solomon as the author. Orthographic analysis from various inscriptions demonstrates that before the tenth century BC Hebrew writing was purely consonantal.[23] Moreover, the copy of Qohelet preserved in the Dead Sea Scrolls is consonantal. This was not the Hebrew writing of the

---

17. Roden, *Elementary Biblical Hebrew*, 14.
18. Roden, *Elementary Biblical Hebrew*, 14–15.
19. Seow, "Linguistic Evidence," 644–45.
20. Sáenz-Badillos, *History of the Hebrew Language*, 16–17.
21. Sáenz-Badillos, *History of the Hebrew Language*, 50.
22. Sáenz-Badillos, *History of the Hebrew Language*, 52.
23. Sáenz-Badillos, *History of the Hebrew Language*, 66.

Historical Context and Background

scribes who copied them. The Scroll dates range from the third century BC to the first century AD.[24] The scribes who copied them from this period, 175 BC for Qohelet, persevered the original Classical Biblical Hebrew (consonantal). In short, some scholars argue that the orthography of the book alone is enough to cast doubt on claims pertaining to the current consensus regarding the late date assigned to Qohelet.[25] There are many technical arguments opposing the view that Qohelet was written early or originally in Classical Biblical Hebrew orthography—examination of structural patterns, phonological and vocabulary comparisons, statistical analysis on linguistic features—spellings, pronoun use, etc. However, the intention of this work was to disavow any notions of Greek influence on Qohelet's philosophy. Thus, priorities have overridden the need to address these technical arguments.

---

24. Leon Levy Dead Sea Scrolls Digital Library.
25. Seow, "Linguistic Evidence," 645, para. 1.

CHAPTER 4

Textual Analysis

דִּבְרֵי קֹהֶלֶת בֶּן־דָּוִד מֶלֶךְ בִּירוּשָׁלָֽם׃

THE HEBREW ABOVE IS how the author begins the book of Ecclesiastes. Translation: "The words of the Teacher, the son of David, king in Jerusalem" (Eccl 1:1). The Hebrew word בֶּן could, according to some scholars, refer to a descendant.[1] However, *The Brown-Driver-Briggs Hebrew and English Lexicon* (BDB) defines it as: noun, masculine, "son."[2] Note, however, most scholars date the text nearly six centuries after Solomon.[3] Nevertheless, if we are to believe the author, he provides more clues to his identity. "I, the Teacher, when king over Israel in Jerusalem, applied my mind to seek and to search out by wisdom all that is under heaven; it is an unhappy business that God has given to human beings to be busy with" (Eccl 1:12–13). This is the first time God is mentioned by Qohelet. However, the spelling and pronunciation is different than the typical usage for God, i.e., יְהֹוָה (*Yahweh*) in the Old Testament. The term for God that Qohelet used, אֱלֹהִים (*elohim*) is a term used less frequently in the Old Testament. Scholars debate the root of the word *elohim* and whether or not it stems from a single origin—originating from

---

1. *New Oxford Annotated Bible*, 947, 1:1 ed. intro.
2. Brown et al., *Brown-Driver-Briggs*, 119, ref. 1121.
3. Alter, *Hebrew Bible*, 679.

either Ugaritic, Phoenician, or possibly Akkadian. אל (*el*) is the Ugaritic term used for god. However, the relationship between the name used for God in Scripture and *el* or *elohim* is disputed. It's interesting that in the Ugaritic text *el* never has the article, which is the same practice used by Qohelet when he uses *elohim*. It appears to be an ancient term used for God that later fell out of common usage. It became popular during the exile when there was a concern for returning to ancient foundations. Job uses it frequently, but in the postexilic books (2 Chronicles, Nehemiah, and Daniel) it is only used a total of five times.[4] Moreover, the Ugaritic text used epithets when referencing El. For example, "the kindly one, El the merciful."[5] This practice parallels with verses in the Old Testament concerning the term: "El of Knowledge" (1 Sam 2:3); "El of glory" (Ps 29:3); and "El of eternity" (Gen 21:33). There is a relationship between Biblical Hebrew and Ugaritic when it comes to how this term was applied. Further, it's worth noting (arguably) that Ugaritic was an early Semitic language. Undisputed, however, is the fact that Ugarit's cuneiform literary text parallel Old Testament poetic style and the kingdom of Ugarit was destroyed in 1200 BC.[6] There are clear parallels, established by Hebraists, between Ugarit and Israel pertaining to literary and cultural contact.[7] The Hebrew orthography used by Qohelet resembles this early Ugaritic text evident by the term used for God.

וְאֵין כָּל־חָדָשׁ תַּחַת הַשָּׁמֶשׁ

There is "nothing new under the sun" (Eccl 1:9). This is a phrase used to signify the mentality of Qohelet's time. As mentioned earlier, the ancients viewed their world as cyclical—having reoccurring cycles of events in history. This view is daunting for the author, nature is an endless, pointless cycle that engulfs generations of humanity with no obvious point. Human sensations do not provide satisfaction for understanding life—there is always a

---

4. Harris et al., *Theological Wordbook*, s.v. "Eloah. God, god" (43n93).
5. Williams, *Basics of Ancient Ugaritic*, 15.
6. Matthews and Benjamin, *Old Testament Parallels*, 358.
7. Sáenz-Badillos, *History of the Hebrew Language*, 33.

31

desire for more. "The eye is not satisfied with seeing, or the ear with hearing" (Eccl 1:8). Neither the accomplishments of humanity, nor the implications, are fully understood or remembered because the ancients have yet to recognize progress within the human race as a whole. Only later generation will reflect on history and recognize a pattern being established, a concept Qohelet cannot comprehend. "The people of long ago are not remembered, nor will there be any remembrance of people yet to come by those who come after them" (Eccl 1:11). There are commentaries, however, which argue the phrase "under the sun" was borrowed from Greek writings, i.e., Homer's *Iliad* (seventh century BC). This argument is unsustainable because the same phrase ("under the sun") occurs in Phoenician inscriptions from the fifth century BC. Thus, according to C. L. Seow, "it cannot be traced exclusively to the Hellenistic period."[8]

רְעוּת רוּחַ

"Chasing after wind" is a term used by Qohelet when he has determined a process or action to be useless or meaningless. The BDB translates רְעוּת as "longing, striving."[9] There are various translations. Nonetheless, the point is, whenever Qohelet used this phrase he was reinforcing his argument—that human activity is unpleasant, futile, and unprofitable, i.e., equivalent to chasing after the wind. "And I have applied my mind to know wisdom and to know madness and folly. I perceived that this also is but a chasing after wind" (Eccl 1:17). As indicated in this verse, Qohelet has pursued many avenues searching for meaning and concludes that all wisdom, madness, and folly is meaningless. He disclosed that there were no limits to his pursuit of pleasure. Yet, when he reflected on his actions the same premise emerged—all is vanity. "I keep my heart from no pleasure, for my heart found pleasure in all my toil, and this was my reward for all my toil. Then I considered all that my hands had done and the toil I had spent in doing it, and again, all was vanity and a chasing after wind" (Eccl 2:10–11). Although, as distraught as he appeared to be in the early chapters,

---

8. Seow, "Linguistic Evidence," 657, para. 1, 3; 658, para. 1.
9. Brown et al., *Brown-Driver-Briggs*, 946, ref. 7469.

glimpses of a solution to his existential crisis are beginning to take hold. This is evident as recorded in the above passage: "for my heart found pleasure in all my toil." The next section will continue with the same approach, textual analysis, but focus will shift more toward the existentialism that developed from Qohelet's evaluation of circumstances pertaining to the human condition.

Proverbs and Poetry

שֶׁמִּקְרֶה אֶחָד יִקְרֶה אֶת־כֻּלָּם

Roughly translated, "the same fate (or chance) happens to them all" (Eccl 2:14). In this passage Qohelet is contemplating the vanity of human achievement. He realizes that the wise and accomplished will perish just the same as the fool. There is also a concern that his heirs may not appreciate the inheritance or legacy he has left them. Perhaps, they will squander it. "Seeing that I must leave it to those who come after me—and who knows whether they will be wise or foolish" (Eccl 2:18–19). Moreover, we see a mentality emerge once again, typical of the ancients regarding over-all quantifiable progress and the inability to contextualize it fully. As explained earlier, for the ancients, there is no transcendent progression for the human race as a whole, that is, nothing will be remembered and continued. (Note, there are exceptions to this mentality seen in other books of the Old Testament dealing with prophecy e.g., messianic prophecy through the Davidian line.) "For there is no enduring remembrance of the wise or of fools, seeing that in the days to come all will have been long forgotten. How can the wise die just like fools?" (Eccl 2:16). That is not to suggest ancient societies did not contribute to a sequence of sustainability. There was, however, a lack of linear thought, i.e., an end goal to human history as their successors—the Christians will attest. Qohelet dedicated the first part of chapter 3 to the cycles of life in poetic format.

> For everything there is a season, and a time for every matter under heaven: a time to be born, and a time to die; a time to plant, and a time to pluck up what is planted; a

time to kill, and a time to heal; a time to break down, and a time to build up; a time to weep, and a time to laugh; a time to mourn, and a time to dance; a time to throw away stones, and a time to gather stones together; a time to embrace, and a time to refrain from embracing; a time to seek, and a time to lose; a time to keep, and a time to throw away; a time to tear, and a time to sew; a time to keep silent, and a time to speak; a time to love, and a time to hate; a time for war, and a time for peace. (Eccl 3:1–8).

Of course, the author's literary work is remembered. Further, depending on the accepted date of the book, the author would be pleased to know his work has been remembered for over two millenniums—even canonized!

אֹהֵב כֶּסֶף לֹא־יִשְׂבַּע כֶּסֶף

The above Hebrew essentially translates: "The lover of money will not be satisfied with money" (Eccl 5:10). In chapter 5 Qohelet used proverbs to critique wealth, possessions, and labor. He compares the accumulation of wealth by the rich and the labor of the poor with the ability to enjoy life. The laborer's hard work, though it provides no wealth, has the benefit of allowing them to sleep, unlike the rich person whose anxiety over the possibility of losing possessions or wealth prevents them from sleeping. "Sweet is the sleep of the laborers, whether they eat little or much; but the surfeit of the rich will not let them sleep" (Eccl 5:12). He recognized that enjoying life is a gift from God. If a person is fortunate enough to gain wealth, avoid economic misfortune, illness, and political disaster; then enjoying simple pleasure from laboring is a gift from God.[10] "This is what I have seen to be good: it is fitting to eat and drink and find enjoyment in all the toil with which one toils under the sun the few days of the life God gives us; for this is our lot. Likewise all to whom God gives wealth and possessions and whom he enables to enjoy them, and to accept their lot and find enjoyment in their toil—this is the gift of God" (Eccl 5:18–19). The theme of finding enjoyment in life through labor and simple pleasure while fearing God is repetitive. In chapter 8, for example, Qohelet's proverbs

---

10. Alter, *Hebrew Bible*, 692.

continue to express the mystery of life and God. However, he concludes that those who fear God have an advantage.

The philosophy in Qohelet's proverbial statements is enigmatic and elusive at times. Still, he acknowledges the importance of revering God even though God's decree is mysterious. "Though sinners do evil a hundred times and prolong their lives, yet I know it will be well with those who fear God, because they stand in fear before him, but it will not be well with the wicked, neither will they prolong their days like a shadow, because they do not stand in fear before God" (Eccl 8:12–13). The final chapter affirms what is expected of humanity. "The end of the matter; all has been heard. Fear God, and keep his commandments; for this is the whole duty of everyone. For God will bring every deed into judgment, including every secret thing, whether good or evil" (Eccl 12:13–14). Most scholars believe the last few verses of the book were added by an editor. Nevertheless, the epilogue, to fear God and keep his commandments, is consistent with Qohelet's teachings.[11] Qohelet's existential philosophy contains an element essential for human race collectively. Whatever a person finds to occupy themselves with must include the acknowledgment of the divinity. Apart from the eternal source from which humanity's morality originates an individual's purpose becomes distorted and society does not function as intended.

---

11. Hankins and Breed, in *New Oxford Annotated Bible*, 959.

Chapter 5

Applications, Imposters, and Fearing God

This section will be concerned primarily with application. It will examine the relevance of Qohelet's philosophy and the relationship between the Western sources responsible for developing philosophies that were integrated into Christian theology. The connection between the decadence of Western morality and secular ideology will be examined. In the process of exploring the mechanisms ancient cultures once used to understand their world a common theme has emerged. In the ancients' recorded history this common theme is the existence of an eternal source—God. The intention in this chapter is to be transparent regarding the application—assigning practicality or a meaning to the philosophy in this study. Categorically, much of the work in this book depends on the philosophy of history—how history is understood and practiced. It is, however, philosophy and not approached strictly from the perspective of a historian. Metaphysical concepts, for example, are connected to the existential philosophy. The theology understood in connection with humanity's place in the world is not popular in many institutions. Thucydides expressed his intention and approach to composing *The Peloponnesian War* in the following sentiment: "It was composed as a permanent legacy, not a show-piece for

Applications, Imposters, and Fearing God

a single hearing."[1] Certainly, the work of the ancient philosophers and theologians used to produce this study would take the same position regarding their work.

Over the course of history, Western nations have replaced their source for morality (God) with institutions—primarily the state. It's difficult to refute the thesis of Aleksandr Solzhenitsyn (see quote in front of book). The West, for the most part, has lost its civic courage, that is, true courage defined by philosophers and theologians examined throughout this study. Perhaps because of the population's unbridled imagination combined with a quest to separate human autonomy from the eternal source that provided the avenue for understanding true morality. The West has organized itself into a pseudo-legalistic fashion focused on transforming society into an egalitarian utopia, rather than promoting moral responsibility and purpose. In short, the West no longer fears God. It has replaced God with institutions resulting in an abomination—causing many of the inhabitants to experience an existential crisis. Considering the recent politically charged events of the twenty-first century, it appears radical secularized efforts will finally achieve the egalitarian system they have strived for—to the extreme. As such, humanity's responsibility to God will continue to be neglected, jeopardizing some of the greatest Western experiments. During the twentieth century, Solzhenitsyn noticed this ideology was beginning to materialize. In his commencement speech at Harvard University, he expressed this anthropocentric ideology well: "There is no evil inherent to human nature. The world belongs to mankind and all the defects of life are caused by wrong social systems, which must be corrected."[2] Essentially, if there is no eternal source to provide humanity with objectifiable morality there could never have been a departure from morality. Thus, the state, in conjunction with various institutions, have vowed to correct society's defects. The problem with egalitarian systems within society is the absence of liberty. The nature of the system itself, forced equality, severely restricts freedom.

---

1. Thucydides, *Peloponnesian War*, 12.
2. Solzhenitsyn, "A World Split Apart," para. 24.

Machiavelli

In chapter 2 Friedrich Nietzsche's philosophy was examined. His repugnance for any notion that humanity was subject to a higher authority produced a philosophy inimical to the human race collectively. However, there exists an ideology equally as destructive to humanity developed by failed diplomate turned political theorist, Niccolò Machiavelli. Machiavelli was born May 3, 1469, in Florence, Italy.[3] Although not much is known of his early life, he was born to a wealthy, prominent family. Machiavelli had a post with an official governing body in Florence. His responsibilities included diplomatic missions and organizing a citizen army. He soon lost his position due to power struggles in Florence between two rival parties. When the Medici family resumed power, Machiavelli was arrested, tortured, and imprisoned on suspicions he conspired against them. Eventually he was released but failed to secure another position within the government. Thus, he spent the rest of his life writing political and military theory, among other things.[4] Machiavelli's theories reflected political, social, and cultural values of his day. He departed from culture conventions and contributed to the decadence of Western politics.

Machiavelli removed Christian values from politics, which was the foundation for humanity's fulfillment at the time. He accomplished this by advancing secularization within politics. Machiavelli's objective was to develop a powerful state. Machiavelli argued that to be successful in politics, occasionally, the abandonment of moral principles was required, and this action was impossible for the traditional Christian because it was in opposition to their theology. Machiavelli's ideas contributed to the strategic positions on statecraft and the acquisition of power rather than on tactics. He was influenced by the classics and based most of his theories on the classical Rome model. Machiavelli inhabited the area where the Renaissance originated—Florence. His theories very much reflected the cultural values of the time.[5] This should not be con-

---

3. Nederman, "Niccolò Machiavelli."
4. Wiesner-Hanks, *Early Modern Europe, 1450–1789*, 135.
5. Nederman, "Niccolò Machiavelli," sect. 4, para. 4.

fused with breaking away from cultural conventions pertaining to Christianity. Machiavelli did break from the cultural norms in that sense, but not in the area of reviving and promoting the classics. Machiavelli offers lessons learned from Rome regarding the republic, such as keeping the citizens in poverty but the government rich. He was also influenced by German cities, praising them, believing some of them were model republics. According to Julie L. Rose, assistant professor at Dartmouth College, in Machiavelli's *Discourses*, he claimed: "After the fall of the Roman Empire the virtue of the world scattered and within Europe remains only with the peoples of Germany today." Machiavelli's writings are a romanticized version of the German people. Further, considering he did not speak German he was probably influenced by Tacitus's *Germania*.[6]

In his publication *The Prince*, Machiavelli argued: "A Prince, therefore, should have no care or thought but for war, and for the regulations and training it requires, and should apply himself exclusively to this and his peculiar province; for war is the sole art looked for in one who rules, and is of such efficacy that it not merely maintains those who are born Princes."[7]

Machiavelli does not specify how war assimilates into the state or what the art of war is that the prince needs to master. Some scholars have suggested these answers can be found in Machiavelli's *Art of War*, which is based on ancient Rome's model of military virtue and the need to return to these concepts in order to overcome modern military corruption and solve the military crisis of sixteenth century Italy. For Machiavelli, virtue is the republic in Rome which he uses as a template for organizing and reconditioning an army. The primary objective is to minimize the danger a soldier poses to the state by making citizens into soldiers. According to Yves Winter, *Art of War* does not offer much to future princes; it turns into a lecture on tactics, better suited for a technical manual rather than a conceptual engagement with the theory of war. Furthermore, according to Winter, some scholars dismiss the book as it becomes dull and tedious the more the work progresses, focusing

---

6. Rose, "Keep the Citizens Poor," 735–37.
7. Machiavelli, *The Prince*, xiv.

on tactics now outdated rather than theory or strategy.[8] Still, other scholars insist that Machiavelli's ideas held their validity over time. For example, according Felix Gilbert, author of *Machiavelli: Renaissance of the Art of War*, Machiavelli's insight on war and the role of the military in society and the questions they produced were not restricted to a specific historical period. Also, to validate a remark mentioned earlier regarding Machiavelli's theories in relation to cultural conventions, Gilbert states, "Machiavelli's attempt to present the Roman military organization as the model for the armies of his time was therefore not regarded as extravagant."[9] Machiavelli's idea of Rome was a utopia, but he may have used chosen facts from Rome's history to validate a picture already created in his mind.[10]

The primary premise in Machiavelli's military strategy in *Art of War* was that the existence of the state depends on its ability to wage war. And "the aim of war is to subject the enemy to your will." To accomplish this task a military campaign must be planned under a unified command by a general upon whom the country bestows its full confidence and trust. However, Machiavelli's conscript idea was not practiced by the following two to three centuries. Instead, the professional soldier was used in war. He also misjudged the importance of equipping the soldiers and the future role of artillery. For example, he was conscious of the financial needs of the military, but he failed to account for the expense of equipping soldiers with firearms. Machiavelli's view of Roman military organization may have caused him to underestimate the importance of new weapons. However, his admiration for Rome led to the development of his Roman model which was fundamental to the role of war in modern times.[11] Carl von Clausewitz, a military strategist who is often critical of other military theorists, argued that Machiavelli showed good judgment in military affairs. He agreed with Machiavelli on his basic points and "that the validity of any special analysis of military

---

8. Winter, "The Prince and His Art of War," 166–68.
9. Gilbert, "Machiavelli," 28–29.
10. Gilbert, "Machiavelli," 22.
11. Gilbert, "Machiavelli," 23, 25–29.

Applications, Imposters, and Fearing God

problems depended on a general perception, on a correct concept of the nature of war."[12]

The fictitious battle in the *Art of War* is eccentric and much of the book is concerned with technical aspects of marching, weaponry, organization, etc. It can be argued that the book also focuses on courage, obedience, and other qualities needed in war. Furthermore, he wrote that the rulers in ancient times inspired their subjects, particularly their soldiers, promoting peace and the fear of God. Yet, in *The Prince*, Machiavelli advocated for none of these qualities. Thus, it's doubtful his writings in *Art of War* represent his true sentiments.[13] Perhaps they need not reflect his true intentions considering he did emphasize the importance of appearances. For example, in *The Prince*, he argued that a ruler does not need morals, only the appearance of morals in the public's view. Essentially, Machiavelli argued that leaders should become imposters of virtue—this would assist them in accomplishing political goals. A mutual theme in both publications is: do whatever necessary to ensure victory both in war and politics. However important Machiavelli's theories were at the time, as warfare became modernized it's clear that military theory extends far beyond organization and making rules for correct battle order. Modern warfare requires an analysis of the events during the course of battle. The entire campaign had to be planned, analyzed, critiqued, and adjusted as the course of action shifted. Machiavelli was no Clausewitz, modern war was much more complex than Machiavelli could have possibly imagined.[14] His work was not in vain, however, as he provided the criteria that future politicians would use for manipulating and controlling society. This ideology exceeded in promoting chicanery for political success. It was a call to depart from the West's philosophy of virtue and courage. Outside of appearances, it discouraged any sincere reverence for a deity, i.e., fearing God. For example, the Greco-Roman philosophy influenced Machiavelli's developmental process relative to his malicious and destructive ideology, but there

---

12 Gilbert, "Machiavelli," 31.
13. Gilbert, "Machiavelli," 24.
14. Gilbert, "Machiavelli," 30.

is an antithetical or inconsistent position between the *Art of War* and *The Prince*. It seems that Machiavelli adopted the traits of virtue as mere tools for manipulation and exploitation (appearances) that he used to persuade the masses into obedience. This is an evil that has continued well into the modern era. Integrate characteristics of virtue and courage into a common religion (or patriotic calling) and economic compensation is less of a necessity for motivation. Perhaps this is because once the militants (professional soldiers or others) are convinced of their duty, the leader has a very efficient and motivated force for securing the state's agenda. It is critical, therefore, that each individual embrace true courage and duty through unadulterated reason, lest they be deceived.

Conclusion

An essential component to sustaining a civilization, society, or empire is to identify and recognize evil. It was hypothesized that providence has a role in society. Providence does not necessarily dictate a civilization's existence, i.e., whether it fails or succeeds, but functions as a continuum transcending established truths to the next phase of the human experience. God may not punish or reward on an individual basis but when the aggregated population within a society becomes corrupt, the historical trend indicates that a collapse in the entire social network is emanate. It seems as if divine laws were integrated within the cosmos and these laws decide the fate of nations based on their collective moral behavior. When virtue and courage has been compromised and distorted through faulty reasoning a nation will no longer fear God. Inevitably, the nation collapses, but the truths pertaining to morality are passed on to another via providence. This is contingent on whether or not the potential nation or civilization is inundated with a fear of God. Life, for the individual, does have meaning. It may be impossible to know the mind of God or why good and bad fortune is experienced capriciously. Nevertheless, ancient philosophy pertaining to morality was integrated into Christian theology giving birth to the linear understanding of history. This worldview has its origins in

Applications, Imposters, and Fearing God

Qohelet's existential philosophy. The inherent value of life resides within the core concepts of the philosophy: To escape vanity, humans must remember their creator, embrace those close to them, find enjoyment in their work, and live a virtuous life by fearing or acknowledging God. Life's mysteries and uncertainties, to a degree, are never fully resolved. The individual, however, can find purpose through relationships and work not as an escape from reality but as an acceptance of their position in a divine enigmatic decree they cannot fully grasp. Fearing God is perhaps the most important trait an individual or nation can possess. This philosophy surpasses the physical—promoting moral behavior as a duty that each individual should practice within their society to ensure the continuation of a civil nation. It transcends through a mechanism understood as providence for the Christians. Moreover, the attributes or developmental habits that result in a virtuous life defined by Aristotle's *Nicomachean Ethics* and exposed in Cicero's philosophy *The Nature of the Gods*, were recognized and refined by Thomas Aquinas under the guidance of Christian Scripture. For example, a moral code was installed in humanity at creation. It was a by-product of God's creation that originated when God created humans in his image. For humans, there exists a relationship between reason and will—each person has the ability to engage their intellect focusing on the morality that dwells within them, enabling them to freely control their will.[15] Unlike the beast, explained by Aristotle, the human was designed with the capacity to reason. In short, each individual has the ability (provided by God) to use reason, rather than succumb to basic instinct, to act responsibly on a moral level. The recognition and acceptance of this philosophy must come to fruition on an individual basis. It cannot be forced on a population by a trendy social movement or a religious institutional creed. Humans must be allowed to freely respond or suppress the moral code installed within them at creation. Otherwise, it becomes a house of cards built on false or insincere morality.

Qohelet's philosophy was not influenced by Hellenistic thought. There may be similarities but there is no evidence that

---

15. Erickson, *Christian Theology*, 275.

the author of Ecclesiastes borrowed from the Greeks to produce his existential philosophy. Perhaps a better candidate of influence came from a source that shared characteristics of this language: Ugarit's cuneiform literary text parallel with the Old Testament's poetic style. Moreover, scholars argue that the orthography of the book alone is enough to cast doubt on claims pertaining to the current consensus regarding the late date assigned to Qohelet. His philosophy contains a component separate from pagan or secular philosophy, i.e., "fear God." It is mostly irrelevant (to this study) whether or not the last few verses of the book were composed by an editor because God was central at an early stage in Qohelet's narrative. Further, this work does no rely on the last few verses to support the thesis. Finally, without an objectifiable source, i.e., God, society regresses to a cluster of distorted abominations susceptible to a miserable existence, "a chasing after the wind," the "vanity of vanities."

Bibliography

Alter, Robert. *The Hebrew Bible: A Translation with Commentary*. Vol. 3, *The Writings*. New York: Norton, 2019.
Aristotle. *Nicomachean Ethics*. Translated by F. H. Peters. New York: Barns & Noble, 2004.
Blue Letter Bible. Website. Last modified January 2021. https://www.blueletterbible.org/.
Brown, Francis, et al. *The Brown-Driver-Briggs Hebrew and English Lexicon*. Peabody: Hendrickson, 2018.
Cicero. *Nature of the Gods*. Translated with introduction by P. G. Walsh. Oxford: Oxford University Press, 2008
Crenshaw, James L. *Ecclesiastes*. Louisville: Westminster John Knox, 1987.
Currid, John D. *Against the Gods*. Wheaton, IL: Crossway, 2013.
Danker, F. W., ed. *A Greek-English Lexicon of the New Testament and Other Early Christian Literature*. 3rd ed. Chicago: University of Chicago Press, 2000.
Elwell, Walter A., ed. *Evangelical Dictionary of Theology*. 2nd ed. Grand Rapids: Baker Academic, 2001.
Erickson, Millard J. *Christian Theology*. 3rd ed. Grand Rapids: Baker Academic, 2013.
Evans, Stephen C., and R. Zachary Manis. *Philosophy of Religion: Thinking about Faith*. Downers Grove: IVP Academic, 2010.
Gilbert, Felix. "Machiavelli: The Renaissance of the Art of War." In *Makers of Modern Strategy: From Machiavelli to the Nuclear Age*, edited by Peter Paret, 11–31. Princeton: Princeton University Press, 1986.
Harris, Laird R., et al. *Theological Wordbook of the Old Testament*. Chicago: Moody, 1980.
Kierkegaard, Søren. *Christianity in Training*. Preface by Richard John Neuhaus. Translated by Walter Lowrie. Edited by John F. Thornton and Susan B. Varenne. New York: Vintage, 2004.
Lemon, M. C. *Philosophy of History: A Guide for Students*. New York: Routledge, 2003.

Bibliography

The Leon Levy Dead Sea Scrolls Digital Library. Last updated 2020. https://www.deadseascrolls.org.il/home.

Long, Gary A. *Grammatical Concepts 101 for Biblical Hebrew*. Grand Rapids: Baker Academic, 2013.

Machiavelli, Niccolò. *The Prince*. Translated by N. H. Thomson. New York: Dover, 1992.

Matthews, Victor H., and Don C. Benjamin. *Old Testament Parallels: Laws and Stories from the Ancient Near East*. 3rd ed. New York: Paulist, 2006.

Nederman, Cary. "Niccolò Machiavelli." In *The Stanford Encyclopedia of Philosophy*, edited by Edward N. Zalta. Summer 2019 ed. https://plato.stanford.edu/archives/sum2019/entries/machiavelli/.

The New Oxford Annotated Bible: New Revised Standard Version with the Apocrypha. Edited by Michael D. Coogan. 5th ed. New York: Oxford University Press, 2018.

Nietzsche, Friedrich. *The Antichrist: A Criticism of Christianity*. 1895. Translated by Anthony M. Ludovici. Introduction by Dennis Sweet. New York: Barns & Noble, 2006.

Pelikan, Jaroslav. "The Image of God." In *Christianity and Classical Culture: The Metamorphosis of Natural Theology in the Christian Encounter with Hellenism*, 120–35. New Haven: Yale University Press, 1993. http://www.jstor.org/stable/j.ctt32bt32.13.

Pinckaers, Servais, et al. "Ethics and the Image of God (1989)." In *The Pinckaers Reader: Renewing Thomistic Moral Theology*, edited by Berkman John and Titus Craig Steven. Washington, DC: Catholic University of America Press, 2005.

Pipes, Richard. *A Concise History of the Russian Revolution*. New York: Vintage, 1996.

Roden, Chet. *Elementary Biblical Hebrew: An Introduction to the Language and Its History*. San Diego: Cognella Academic, 2009.

Rose, Julie L. "'Keep the Citizens Poor': Machiavelli's Prescription for Republican Poverty." *Political Studies* 64 (October 2016) 734–47. https://doi-org.ezproxy.liberty.edu/10.1111/1467-9248.12204.

Sáenz-Badillos, Angel. *A History of the Hebrew Language*. New York: Cambridge University Press, 1996.

Schniedewind, William M., and Joel H. Hunt. *A Primer on Ugaritic: Language, Culture, and Literature*. New York: Cambridge: Cambridge University Press, 2007.

Schreiner, Thomas R. *The King in His Beauty: A Biblical Theology of the Old and New Testaments*. Grand Rapids: Baker Academic, 2013.

Seow, C. L. "Linguistic Evidence and the Dating of Qohelet." *Journal of Biblical Literature* 115 (Winter 1996) 643–66. https://www.jstor.org/stable/3266347.

Solzhenitsyn, Alexandr. "A World Split Apart." Delivered June 8, 1978, Harvard University. Available at *American Rhetoric: Online Speech Bank*. https://www.americanrhetoric.com/speeches/alexandersolzhenitsynharvard.htm.

Bibliography

Spawforth, A. J. S. *Greece and the Augustan Cultural Revolution.* Cambridge: Cambridge University Press, 2012.

Strong, James. "Hebrew Strong's Dictionary." *Accordance English Study Software,* version 3.1, 2013.

Thucydides. *The Peloponnesian War.* Translated by Martin Hammond. Introduction by P. J. Rhodes. New York: Oxford University Press, 2009.

Tillich, Paul. *The Courage to Be.* 3rd ed. New Haven: Yale University Press, 2014.

Walsh, P. G., trans. *Nature of the Gods.* Introduction by P. G. Walsh. New York: Oxford University Press, 2008.

Walton, John H., et al. *The IVP Bible Background Commentary: Old Testament.* Downers Grove: IVP Academic, 2000.

Wiesner-Hanks, Merry E. *Early Modern Europe, 1450–1789.* 2nd ed. Cambridge: Cambridge University Press, 2013.

Williams, Michael. *Basics of Ancient Ugaritic: A Concise Grammar, Workbook, and Lexicon.* Grand Rapids: Zondervan Academic, 2012.

Winter, Yves. "The Prince and His Art of War: Machiavelli's Military Populism." *Social Research* 81 (2014) 165–91. https://www.jstor.org/stable/26549606.

Index

abyss, of Nietzsche, ix
advantage, of those who fear God, 35
afterlife, 8
Alexander the Great, 27
all as vanity, for Qohelet, 32
analytic philosophy of history, 6
ancient philosophy, xii–xiv
The Antichrist (Nietzsche), 12
anxiety, 3, 34
appearances, Machiavelli emphasizing, 41
Aquinas, Thomas, 2, 3, 16, 43
aristocratic values, associated with courage, 2–3
Aristotle, xii–xiii, 2, 5, 10, 13
Art of War (Machiavelli), 39, 40, 41, 42

Baal, in Ugaritic literature, 9
beasts, 2, 13
beginning of knowledge, "the fear of the Lord" as the cause of, 23

Cappadocian Fathers, 18
causation, notion of absent in the ancients' view, 8
character, no bearing on one's fortune, xiii
"a chasing after the wind," 26, 32–33

Christian religion, connections to the Old Testament, 9
Christian theologians, on choices, 1
Christian theology, on the source of morality, x
Christian thinkers, applied Aristotle's principles, 10
Christian values, removed from politics, 38
Christianity, 12, 13
    viewing history as linear, 7
Cicero, xii, xiii, 26
circumstance: Cause, examples in English, 23
citizens, making into soldiers, 39
civilization, providence not guaranteeing, 15
Classical Biblical Hebrew, 28, 29
classics, Machiavelli reviving and promoting, 39
Clausewitz, Machiavelli was no, 41
conscience, providence working with, 15
Contingency (condition) grouping example, 23
cosmos, God created, 10
courage. *See also* true courage
    as the ability to reason, 3–4
    concepts of, 3
    as an ethical reality, 1–2

49

Index

courage (*continued*)
    making economic
        compensation less of a
        necessity, 42
The Courage to Be (Tillich), 1
cultural conventions, Machiavelli's
    theories in relation to, 40
cuneiform literary text, of Ugarit, 31
cycles
    ancients trapped in reoccuring,
        10, 27, 31
    of events reoccurring in
        history, 7
    of life in poetic format, 33–34
    in nature as unpredictable for
        Qohelet, 21
    regularities as, 8
cyclical fatalism, 14

danger, of a soldier to the state, 39
date, of the composition of
    Ecclesiastes, 20
Dead Sea Scrolls, Biblical Hebrew
    in, 28
death, x, 21–22
deceptive philosophy, of Nietzsche,
    12
deity, in a God-fearing society, 18
desire, reason distinguishing
    natural and unnatural, 4
Discourses (Machiavelli), 39
duty, 42

Ecclesiastes. *See also* Qohelet
    assigned to wisdom literature, 20
    attributed to Solomon, xi
    author of, 27, 30
    beginning words of, 30
    decided on as a title by the
        Septuagint translators, xi
    focus on, ix
"elect" orthodox Christians,
    viewing history as linear, 7

elohim, ancient term used for God,
    30–31
enjoying life, as a gift from God, 34
Enoch, presented with an
    alternative to Sheol, 22
essence, 1, 2, 5
eternal consequences, of the
    pursuit of desires, 26
eternal source
    in the ancients' recorded
        history, 36
    an individual's purpose
        distorted apart from, 35
    necessity of an, ix
    recognizing, 21
ethics, integrated with Christian
    theology, x
Evans, C. Stephen, 19
events, ancients not attempting to
    understand, 8
everyone, same fate coming to, xiv
evil, identifying and recognizing, 42
existence, preceding essence, 1
existential problem, 13
existentialism
    determining meaning to life, 4
    developed from Qohelet's
        evaluation of
        circumstances, 33
    finding meaning, 1
    of Qohelet advocating for
        pursuing pleasure, 22
existentialists, choosing a purpose, 5

fables, compared to myths, 7
faithfulness, of those fearing the
    Lord, 25
false mentalities, should not be
    condemned, 8
fate, 14, 33
"fear," derivation of the word, 22
fear and rage, driving beasts to
    rush into danger, 13
fear of the Lord, 22, 24–25

Index

fearing God
    as consistent with Qohelet's teachings, 35
    Machiavelli discouraged any, 41
    as the most important trait of an individual or nation, 43
    as not about extending one's life, 22
    putting the human condition into perspective, 24
firearms, Machiavelli failed to account for, 40
"forbidden courage," Nietzsche propagated, 12
forced equality, restricting freedom, 37
free will, 15, 16
future generations, looking back at the scientific era, 26

German cities, Machiavelli influenced by, 39
Germania (Tacitus), 39
Gilbert, Felix, 40
God
    enabling humanity to look forward, 10
    first time mentioned by Qohelet, 30
    of the Hebrews depicted as transcendent, 9
    as a moral being, 19
    no one attributing virtue to, xiii
    not punishing or rewarding on an individual basis, 42
    replaced with institutions, 37
gods, of Near Eastern culture having limits, 9
Greco-Roman philosophy, influenced Machiavelli, 41–42
Greek language, impact on late Jewish communities, 20
Greeks, view of history, 10
Gregory of Nazianzus, 18–19
Gregory of Nyssa, 18

happiness, virtuous living resulting in, xiii
hard work, of the laborer allowing them to sleep, 34
Hebrew (Biblical), 28, 29, 31
Hebrew word "Qohelet," Greek word Ecclesiastes substituted for, 20
Hebrew-English Lexicon (BDB), English words for fear, 23
hedonists, 25, 27
Hellenistic culture, shift in mentality, 8–9, 27
heroic-aristocratic ethics, of the early Middle Ages, 3
historical context and background, of the book of Ecclesiastes, 20–29
history
    as linear, 10, 42–43
    "making sense" of, 6
    providence and patterns in, 14–19
    reoccurring cycles of events in, 7, 31
human achievement, vanity of, 33
human activity, as chasing after the wind, 32
human affairs, xiv, 17
human condition, xii, 5
human nature, setting societies on the path to destruction, 14
human sensations, understanding life and, 31–32
humanity
    going in circles along with nature, 8
    needing an objectifiable reference, xii
    Nietzsche's contempt for, 12

humanity (*continued*)
   humanity no transcendent progression for the ancients, 33
   providing with a meaningful past, 10
   reason distorted by Christianity, 12
   seeking to understand order in the universe, 25
   trapped in a cycle of reoccurrences, 27
   wandered furthest from instincts, 13
humans
   believed in the existence of a higher reality, 16
   capacity to make ethical choices, 17
   with the capacity to reason, 43
   created in God's image, 9, 16, 43
   must remember their creator to escape vanity, 43
   regarding as physical entities, 17
   as solely responsible for their acts, xiii
humility, not an attribute embraced by Nietzsche, 12

identity, not hinging on occupation, 5
image of God, 16, 17, 18–19
imaginations, unrestrained, 25–26
imposters of virtue, leaders becoming, 41
individuals
   failing to enjoy life, 25
   finding purpose through relationships and work, 43
   obligation to practice virtue and self-discipline, 15
inequalities, limited power to correct, 21
instinct, humanity's most trusted characteristic, 13
intellectual life, focusing on reason and will, 16
intellectual mediation, 7
intelligentsia, 17, 18
Isaiah, criticizing Baalism, 9

Jehovah, pronunciation unknown until 1520, 23
Jewish custom, to destroy copies of manuscripts, 28
Job, 21, 31
Judeo-Christian monotheism and understanding of time, implications for existential philosophy, 9–10

"keep my commandments and you will live," as a value statement but not a promise, 24
Kierkegaard, Søren, 4
knights, represented courage, 3
knowing, processes for, 7
knowledge, 23, 24

laboring, as a gift from God, 34
Late Biblical Hebrew, written after the exile, 28
late Persian or early Hellenistic periods, economic and cultural shifts associated with, 27
Lemon, M. C., 5, 6, 7–8
liberty, absence of with egalitarian systems, 37
life
   enjoying, 25
   inherent value of, 43
   meaningless without an objectifiable source, 26
   as mere breath (short), 25

Index

linear thought, lack of for the ancients, 33
living rationally, through intellect, xiii
Livy, 15
"Lord," derivation of the word, 22
lover of money, 34

Machiavelli, Niccolò, 38–42
Machiavelli: Renaissance of the Art of War (Gilbert), 40
Masoretic text, of the Hebrew Bible, 28
meaning, Qohelet searching for, 32
meaning of life
　assigning, 5, 26
　dismissing on a priori grounds, 6
　questions associated with, 7
meaningful existence, 1
"mere breath," Hebrew word for vanity meaning, xi
messianic prophecy, through the Davidian line, 33
metaphysical concepts, existential philosophy and, 36
methods, of understanding the world, 26
military campaign, planning, 40
military connection, with the word "courage," 2
modern warfare, requiring an analysis of the events, 41
moderns, understanding the world through observation and rational thought, 7
money, lover of, 34
moral behavior, 42, 43
moral code, 18, 43
moral decadence, of Greek and Roman civilizations, 15
moral obligations, connection to God, 18
moral philosophy, x, xii

moral virtue, developing habits of, xiii
morality, 13, 16–19, 42
multiplier effect, of a propaganda campaign, 17
mythical stories, 7, 8, 9

nations, fate of based on collective moral behavior, 42
natural desire, as limited, 4
nature, 7, 18
Nature of the Gods (Cicero), xiii, 43
Near East, all societies polytheist, except Hebrew, 9
Near Eastern beliefs, pertaining to the netherworld or Sheol, 22
New Science (Vico), 14
Nicomachean Ethics (Aristotle), xii, 15, 43
Nietzsche, Elisabeth, as Nietzsche's editor, 11
Nietzsche, Franziska, 11
Nietzsche, Friedrich, ix, 11, 14, 38
nihilism, Nietzsche on, 14
nobility, courage as a characteristic of, 3
"nothing new under the sun," 31

obedience, of those fearing the Lord, 25
objectifiable source, 16, 26, 44
obligation, to enjoy life, 25
occupation, giving meaning to life, 5
Old Testament, authors view of their world, 9
"the one who assembles," as the meaning of Ecclesiastes, xi
original sin, nearly destroyed the image of God in humanity, 16
origins, of morality, 16–19

Index

pagan myths, polemical theory used to counter, 9
the past, ancients' understanding of, 7
patterns, occurring throughout history, 14
The Peloponnesian War (Thucydides), 36–37
perspectives, proverbs representing true, 24
philosophy
    of Aristotle, 2
    existential, 9–10
    Greco-Roman, 41–42
    of history, 5–7, 36
    as a method to understand the world, 26
    moral, x, xii–xiv
    Nietzsche's deceptive, 12
    of Qohelet not influenced by Hellenistic thought, 43–44
    subjective approach pertaining to Greek, 27
Phoenician writing system, 28
phylakes (guardians), *thymoeides* related to, 2
Pipes, Richard, 17
pity, making a person defective, 12
Platonic thought, sociological developments of, 2
pleasure, 4, 22, 25, 33
"pleasure principle," of the Stoics, 3
poetic format, cycles of life in, 33–34
political agenda, Nietzsche's work supporting, 11
politicians, 17, 41
politics, requiring abandonment of moral principles, 38
power, acquisition of, 38
primal instincts, Nietzsche advocating for, 13
The Prince (Machiavelli), 39, 41
progress
    ancients having no concept of, 7, 8, 32
    concept of as a whole for the human race, 10
    enabled the linear understanding of history, 14
progressive science, 17
proverbs, 24, 34
Proverbs (Book of), 21, 22, 23
providence, 14, 15

Qohelet. *See also* Ecclesiastes
    on all things as wearisome, 3
    attempting to date the text of, 27
    copy of preserved in the Dead Sea Scrolls, 27–29
    on God's disposition as unknowable, 21
    on the meaningless and absurdity in life, 3
    mentioning God's judgment, 26
    no distinction between beasts and humans, 21
    not attempting to predict events, 21
    not recognizing a pattern in history, 32
    notions of Greek influence on, 29
    philosophy of, 44
    promoted "the fear of the Lord," 22
    on the same fate coming to all, xiii–xiv
    as the untranslated Hebrew word for Ecclesiastes, xii
    used *elohim* for God, 30
    warning for those who pursued their desires, 25–26
    in the Writings portion of the Hebrew Bible, 28
Qohelet (as author), 21, 25

Index

radical secularized efforts, 37
rage, not real courage, 2
rational-democratic ethics, 3
reason
    bringing existentialism to its logical conclusion, 5
    distinguishing humans from beasts, 21
    each individual having the ability to use, 43
    as humanity's essential nature, 4
    right action performing through, xiii
    uniting with will to produce free will, 16
regularities, 8, 14
relationship, between reason and will, 43
religion
    answering existential questions, 6–7
    as a method to understand the world, 26
reverence for God, 24, 35
right action, performing through reason, xiii
Roman Empire, ability to sustain discipline, 15
Roman model, of Machiavelli, 40
Roman writers, noticing societal shifts, 15
Romans, view of history, 10
Rome, Machiavelli offering lessons learned from, 39
Rose, Julie L., 39
ruler, needing only the appearance of morals, 41

sacrifice of life, as the greatest test of courage, 2
Sartre, Jean-Paul, xii
scholars, on use of the Hebrew word Qohelet, 20
science, 6, 17, 26
secular existentialism, meaning of having no value, 27
secular externalism, inefficiencies in the philosophy of, 26–27
secularization, Machiavelli advancing within politics, 38
seeds of discontent, taking root if followed by a multiplier effect, 17
self-sacrifice, 4, 13
Seow, C. L., 32
Septuagint, Ecclesiastes as the title, 20
social justice movements, 14
societal ethics, the image of God key to, 18–19
society
    God-fearing, 18
    reorganizing and avoiding destructive paths, 14
    restructuring, 17
    transforming, 37
soldiers, ready to sacrifice life, 2
Solomon, as the author of Ecclesiastes, xi, 27, 28
Solzhenitsyn, Aleksandr, 37
son, word translated as, 30
"son of David," as author of Ecclesiastes, xi
specialist studies of history, 5–6
speculative philosophy of history, 5, 6
the state, 37, 40
Stoics, 3, 25
strong person, as the typical villain, 12
subjective approach, pertaining to Greek philosophy, 27
suicide, 3
sun, ancients' belief that it orbited the earth, 8
superstition, as a method to understand the world, 26

Index

the Teacher, searching out by wisdom, 30
text, date and influence of Qohelet, 27–29
textual analysis, of Ecclesiastes, 30–35
those who fail to fear the Lord, 24
thought process, pertaining to human origins and the passing of time, 9
Thucydides, 36–37
thymoeides, combination of courage and *thymós*, 2
Tillich, Paul, 1–2, 3, 5
time, cyclical versus linear understanding of, 7–10
a time, for every matter under heaven, 33–34
true courage. *See also* courage
    according to Aristotle, 13
    critical that each individual embrace, 42
    defined by philosophers and theologians, 37
    as a derivative of reason, 5
truth, 4, 7, 42

Ugaritic, as an early Semitic language, 31
Ugaritic cuneiform literary text, 44
Ugaritic literature, 9
"under the sun," xii, 32
understanding, 23
United States, as an improved political system, 16
universal history, 5
unnatural desire, as unlimited, 4
unrestrained imaginations, 25–26

vanity
    bringing into question the meaning of life, 4
    of human achievement, 33
    humans escaping, 43
    as the key word in Ecclesiastes, xi
    for Qohelet, 32
venturing courage, 3
Vico, Giambattista, 14
victory, ensuring, 41
virtue, 39, 42
virtuous acts, repetitively performing, xiii
virtuous life, living, 10, 43
von Clausewitz, Carl, 40–41
vowel system, Jewish scholars developed, 28

war, 39, 41
the wealthy, unlimited desires of, 4
the West, no longer fearing God, 37
Western politics, Machiavelli contributed to the decadence of, 38
the wicked, not standing in fear before God, 35
"will to power," as humanity's strength, 12
Winter, Yves, 39–40
wisdom, 2, 23
wisdom courage, representing "strength of mind," 3
wisdom literature, genre of, 20–21
wise and accomplished, perishing just the same as the fool, 33
work, finding enjoyment in, 43
world, of the ancients as animated, 7

Yahweh, 9, 23

www.ingramcontent.com/pod-product-compliance
Lightning Source LLC
Chambersburg PA
CBHW071750040426
42446CB00012B/2515